The Kefaya Movement

A Case Study of a Grassroots Reform Initiative

T0303116

Nadia Oweidat, Cheryl Benard, Dale Stahl, Walid Kildani,
Edward O'Connell, Audra K. Grant

Prepared for the Office of the Secretary of Defense
Approved for public release; distribution unlimited

RAND NATIONAL DEFENSE RESEARCH INSTITUTE

The research described in this report was prepared for the Office of the Secretary of Defense (OSD). The research was conducted in the RAND National Defense Research Institute, a federally funded research and development center sponsored by the OSD, the Joint Staff, the Unified Combatant Commands, the Department of the Navy, the Marine Corps, the defense agencies, and the defense Intelligence Community under Contract W74V8H-06-C-0002.

Library of Congress Cataloging-in-Publication Data

Oweidat, Nadia.
The Kefaya movement : a case study of a grassroots reform initiative / Nadia Oweidat ...[et al.]
p. cm.
Includes bibliographical references.
ISBN 978-0-8330-4548-5 (pbk. : alk. paper)
1. Kifayah (Organization) 2. Opposition (Political science)—Egypt. 3. Egypt—Politics and government—1981– I. Title.

JQ3831.O84 2008
322.4'40962—dc22

2008043735

The RAND Corporation is a nonprofit research organization providing objective analysis and effective solutions that address the challenges facing the public and private sectors around the world. RAND's publications do not necessarily reflect the opinions of its research clients and sponsors.

Published 2008 by the RAND Corporation
1776 Main Street, P.O. Box 2138, Santa Monica, CA 90407-2138
1200 South Hayes Street, Arlington, VA 22202-5050
4570 Fifth Avenue, Suite 600, Pittsburgh, PA 15213-2665
RAND URL: http://www.rand.org/
To order RAND documents or to obtain additional information, contact
Distribution Services: Telephone: (310) 451-7002;
Fax: (310) 451-6915; Email: order@rand.org

Preface

This monograph is part of the RAND National Security Research Division's Alternative Strategy Initiative, sponsored by the Rapid Reaction Technology Office in the Office of the Undersecretary of Defense for Acquisition, Technology, and Logistics. The Alternative Strategy Initiative includes research on creative use of the media, radicalization of youth, civic involvement to stem sectarian violence, the provision of social services to mobilize aggrieved sectors of indigenous populations, and the topic of this volume, alternative movements.

This study looks at an indigenous movement for political reform in the Arab world and its implications for U.S. policy in the region. Specifically, it documents the history of the Egyptian Movement for Change, also known as Kefaya (*kefaya* is the Arabic word for *enough*). It examines Kefaya's birth, its accomplishments, and the reasons for its decline through an analysis of the work of Egyptian scholars and Arabic-language media reports (including online and new media), as well as structured interviews conducted in February and May 2007 with persons associated with and observers of Kefaya and the Muslim Brotherhood. This research should be of interest to persons interested in the challenges to grassroots attempts to bring about democracy and implement political reform in the Arab world in general and in Egypt in particular.

This research was sponsored by the Office of the Undersecretary of Defense for Acquisition, Technology, and Logistics and conducted within the International Security and Defense Policy Center of the RAND National Defense Research Institute, a federally funded research and development center sponsored by the Office of the Secretary of Defense, the Joint Staff, the Unified Combatant Commands, the Department of the Navy, the Marine Corps, the defense agencies, and the defense Intelligence Community. The research also builds on work conducted by the Alternative Strategy Initiative.

For more information on RAND's International Security and Defense Policy Center, contact the Director, James Dobbins. He can be reached by email at dobbins@rand.org; by phone at 703-413-1100, extension 5134; or by mail at the RAND Corporation, 1200 South Hayes Street, Arlington, Virginia 22202-5050. For more information on the Alternative Strategy Initiative, contact Cheryl Benard. She can be reached by mail at benard@rand.org or phone at 703-413-1100, extension 5679. More information about RAND is available at www.rand.org.

Contents

Preface ... iii
Summary ... vii
Acknowledgments ... xiii

CHAPTER ONE
Introduction ... 1

CHAPTER TWO
Kefaya's Origins ... 3
The U.S.-Egyptian Relationship ... 4
Democratization in Egypt During the 1990s ... 8
Emergence of Kefaya ... 10

CHAPTER THREE
Kefaya's Successes ... 17
Timing and Simplicity of Message ... 18
Position to Mobilize and Form Coalitions ... 18
Setting an Example of Peaceful Opposition ... 19
Successful Exploitation of Information Technology ... 20
Kefaya's Internet Strategy ... 22
  Bloggers ... 23
  General Public ... 23
  Media ... 24
Challenging the Regime ... 24
Inspiration for Others: Kefaya's National and International Influence ... 25

CHAPTER FOUR
Kefaya's Decline 27
Intimidation by the State 27
Manipulation of "Reform" Laws 30
State-Controlled Media 31
The Faltering of the Coalition with the Islamists 32
Problems with the Elite and the Antidemocracy Message 35
Internal Reasons for Kefaya's Decline 38
Lessons for a Future Kefaya 40

CHAPTER FIVE
Conclusions and Implications for U.S. Policy 43
Perceptions of the United States 44
Policy Recommendations 48
Conclusion 52

References 55

Summary

The United States has professed an interest in greater democratization in the Arab world, particularly since the September 2001 attacks by terrorists from Saudi Arabia, the United Arab Emirates, Egypt, and Lebanon. This intrest has been part of an effort to reduce destabilizing political violence and terrorism. As President George W. Bush noted in a 2003 address to the National Endowment for Democracy, "As long as the Middle East remains a place where freedom does not flourish, it will remain a place of stagnation, resentment, and violence ready for export" (The White House, 2003). The United States has used varying means to pursue democratization, including a military intervention that, though launched for other reasons, had the installation of a democratic government as one of its end goals.

However, indigenous reform movements are best positioned to advance democratization in their own country. This monograph examines one such movement, the Egyptian Movement for Change, commonly known as Kefaya (*kefaya* is the Arabic word for *enough*). At first, Kefaya successfully mobilized wide segments of Egyptian society, but later it proved unable to overcome many impediments to its reform efforts and political participation.

This monograph examines Kefaya's birth, its accomplishments, and the challenges that led to its decline to better understand why reform has not taken hold in Egypt. For a broader context, it also reviews the recent history of Egyptian politics, including U.S.-Egyptian relations, and perceptions of the role of the United States in advancing democracy in the region. It relies on analyses of the work of Egyptian scholars and Arabic-language media reports.

The Context: U.S.-Egyptian Relations

The relationship between the United States and the Arab Republic of Egypt has undergone a two-fold transformation in recent decades. First, and perhaps most significantly, the United States has come to consider Egypt a significant strategic ally in the region. This view stems from the efforts of Egyptian President Anwar Sadat during the 1970s to reposition Egypt to favor the West, giving the United States another option in its efforts to contain the ambitions of the Soviet Union in the region. It was further boosted by the negotiation of a formal peace between Egypt and Israel, making Egypt and the United States partners in securing stability in the region. The relationship deepened further after the Cold War, with Egypt aiding the United States in its military activity in the region, including occasional use of Egyptian air bases and access to Egyptian air space for transiting U.S. forces.

Second, although the United States has sought political reform within Egypt as a means to promote political stability there, it has been reluctant to take some concrete actions to push Egypt toward democratization. In part as a result of this reluctance, by some accounts Egypt was less democratic in 2001 than it was in 1981, when Hosni Mubarak succeeded to the presidency.

Kefaya's Origins and Initial Success

President Mubarak's eventual desire for an unprecedented fifth six-year term to begin in 2005 and the possible succession of his son Gamal Mubarak to the presidency led to discontent within Egypt, culminating in the emergence of Kefaya. Kefaya united several political parties in demand for rotation of power. Although it did not have the financial network of organizations such as the Muslim Brotherhood, the media platforms available to the state, or the legacy many older parties enjoyed, it helped focus discontent on the Mubarak regime. To do so, Kefaya employed means not previously seen in Egyptian politics, means that may have some promise for future democratic movements.

There are several reasons for Kefaya's initial success. First, it kept its message simple. Its very name, "enough," crystallized Egyptian frustration with the government. Its slogan, *la lil-tawrith, la lil-tamdid* [no to inheritance, no to extension], helped focus public attention in Egypt on the issue of hereditary rule raised by Mubarak's plans. Kefaya presented a simple analysis of the situation that any citizen could understand.

Second, Kefaya was able to unite diverse groups in its pursuit of broadly acceptable democratic reforms. It appealed to reform-minded individuals and parties of all social backgrounds and political persuasions. Its peaceful demonstrations were also appealing in a Middle East ravaged by extremism.

Third, Kefaya ably exploited information technology. It used electronic messages, including text messages between cell phone users, to publicize its rallies among members and the general public. It pursued a multifaceted Internet strategy to disseminate its message. It published advertisements online, finding these to be more effective than print advertisements in publications the authorities could confiscate. It propagated banners and political cartoons using its own Web page and those of sympathetic bloggers. It documented abuses by state security officers using digital photography and distributed the images online.

Kefaya leaders see their greatest accomplishment as having broken down the population's aversion to direct confrontation with the regime. Prior to the Kefaya movement, Egyptians never dared to openly oppose their government. Kefaya has also inspired other social reform movements, particularly those of workers, in Egypt, and similar reform movements in other nations.

Causes of Kefaya's Decline

Though succeeding where others had not, Kefaya eventually faltered in the face of intimidation by the state, as had earlier movements. State security agents harassed and abused Kefaya members. The government also manipulated reform laws to thwart democratization. The constitutional amendment allowing multiple candidates for president, for example, also made it virtually impossible for any candidate to run without the approval of the ruling party.

Although Kefaya was adept in its use of electronic media, the more prevalent state-controlled media managed to overwhelm Kefaya's message. Leading Egyptian newspapers insinuated that Kefaya's leaders were traitors who were carrying out orders from the U.S. government to undermine the stability of the country. Egypt's government-owned press continued to be blatant in its bias for the ruling party.

One of Kefaya's early strengths, its ability to work with all parties, including Islamists, eventually contributed to its decline. Ideological differences divided Kefaya from Islamists. For example, when some secular Kefaya leaders supported a statement by the Minister of Culture against the wearing of *hijab*, many Islamist senior leaders withdrew from the movement, decrying it as an attack against Islam. More generally, Islamist and secular leaders within the movement had differing interpretations of democracy, with these varying notions underlying fissures between them.

Other internal conflicts also led to the decline of the movement. Political parties that had joined with Kefaya in pursuit of common goals eventually jostled for position within it. The political-reform goals of the movement also may have been too far removed from the concerns of average Egyptians, most of who live in or near poverty. Some support also fell away over concern that Kefaya had no goals beyond its opposition to Mubarak.

Lessons for Reform Movements and the United States

The challenges that Kefaya and other reform movements in the Middle East have faced, and that the United States may face in supporting them, point to several policy options.

First, the United States should urge authoritarian regimes in the Middle East to initiate democratic reform in a consistent and unambiguous fashion. This would send a clear signal over time to both the regimes and populations of the Middle East that while the United States values its long-standing partnerships in the region, it equally values those that are moving toward greater freedom for their citizens. The United States should also develop a means of identifying incipient democratic initiatives so that it can facilitate their growth and guide them toward viable and constructive action.

Second, the United States should develop the means to better assess and understand local political conditions and to support the reform movements emerging from them. Although Islamist opposition movements present a challenge to the United States, they sometimes have the most credibility with the local population. The United States should help protect all reform movements that eschew violence and seek peaceful change away from politics based on repression and intimidation. It can also help reform movements develop their own international or transnational messages. Kefaya imitators in other nations, for example, could help the movement re-emerge as a transnational one that is less susceptible to pressure from any one government.

Third, the United States should also recognize that nongovernmental organizations have an important role to play in fostering democratic change, particularly in efforts to mediate between groups and train organizers. It would be best if these nongovernmental organizations were created within rather than outside Egypt. The United States can play a role in encouraging such organizations and protecting their right to function.

Fourth, the United States should help reformers obtain and use information technology. The ability of Egyptian activists to document and expose human-rights abuses forced the government to prosecute some of the perpetrators of such acts. Disseminating the messages of reformers in international online forums can also help thwart state repression of reformers.

Fifth, the United States should help reformers foster effective social-service programs that offer practical help to the peoples of their nations to make inroads into areas that have been increasingly claimed by antidemocratic organizations. Offering education, health care, and financial support to the population can help build strong grassroots relationships, relationships that may be later leveraged into political support and recruitment.

Acknowledgments

The authors are thankful for the support of our sponsors, including Benjamin Riley, director of the Rapid Reaction Technology Office in the Office of the Undersecretary of Defense for Acquisition, Technology, and Logistics, and Richard Higgins and Chris Dufour, both of the Irregular Warfare Support Branch in the Office of the Assistant Secretary of Defense for Special Operations/Low-Intensity Conflict and Interdependent Capabilities. We also benefited from the support and encouragement of James Dobbins, director of RAND's International Security and Defense Policy Center. We thank our colleagues Michael Lostumbo, Angel Rabasa, Clifford Grammich, and Francisco Walter for all their help with this project. Finally, we thank the contributors to this monograph who prefer to remain anonymous.

CHAPTER ONE

Introduction

Much of the Middle East is governed by repressive regimes. Many of these autocratic regimes are consistently confronted by opposition movements that seek to bring about democratic reforms. These movements, however, operate under significant difficulties and assisting them in any tangible fashion is not easy.

Opposition movements in the Middle East are regularly repressed, sometimes brutally. Many persons in these nations may be intimidated by or unaccustomed to political engagement, which, in such settings, is not a commonplace civic activity but a high-risk enterprise.

Yet as a result of poverty, underdevelopment, and ineffective governance, much of the population needs social support. In the absence of well-functioning government agencies, such support is often provided by social movements. In many cases, Islamist organizations have proven most adept stepping in to fill this need; they later leverage the population's appreciation for the social services they provide for political gain.

By contrast, more-mainstream secular reform movements have been less successful in developing popular support. They lack the Islamists' financial resources and their networks outside the political arena. While secular groups focus on politics, Islamist groups provide a variety of essential services that attract a loyal constituency. Secularists expect to enjoy a following based only on political views without investing much effort in constituency building. As a result, with the exception of some public demonstrations, they have not been good at broadening their base of support.

In some instances, secular reform movements have sought pragmatic coalitions with Islamists. These coalitions were deemed necessary to reduce vulnerability to government repression and to broaden support. Such broad coalitions sought strength in numbers by uniting around near-term goals for political change while postponing the resolution of differences on the nature and direction of the movement. Secular movements also considered joining forces with religious groups as a means to appeal beyond their usual base of intellectuals and middle-class professionals. Such movements ultimately tend to be short-lived.

In this monograph, we examine a grassroots movement in the Middle East and discuss the opportunities that such a movement offers to those seeking democratization in the region. Kefaya was unique among democratization movements in the Middle East in that it brought together modern-day radicals and moderates from various ideological currents and in its success in forming alliances with other, diverse movements. We also focus on Kefaya because of its geography: Egypt has had a long and close relationship with the United States, which might therefore be able to effectively exert some political pressure for democratization on Egypt.

CHAPTER TWO

Kefaya's Origins

The Kefaya movement began in the autumn of 2004, catapulting into Egyptian politics after launching what is considered the first major anti-Mubarak demonstration ever. The catalyst for the organization's creation was the impending 2005 presidential elections in Egypt. At stake were issues related to the persistence of authoritarian rule and the inheritance of presidential power. Eventually, Kefaya's platform expanded to include additional grievances from other quarters. Whether Kefaya was truly a new movement or an alternative mechanism for a collection of groups to air grievances is open to debate. Regardless, its unique characteristics, as noted, make it worth extensive analysis. These include both its placement in Egypt (with which the United States has had a long and close relationship and might therefore be expected to influence), its search for a middle path between an often repressive government on one side and radical Islamists on the other, and its use of information technology and new media.

At first, Kefaya successfully mobilized wide segments of Egyptian society, but it later proved unable to overcome many impediments to reform and political participation. In this and subsequent chapters, we examine Kefaya's birth, its accomplishments, and the circumstances that led to its decline. We begin by reviewing the historical context of the movement, a context that includes both U.S.-Egyptian relations and recent Egyptian political affairs.

The U.S.-Egyptian Relationship

For several decades, relations between the United States and the Arab Republic of Egypt were shaped by the experiences and mindset of the Cold War. In particular, Egypt sought the patronage of the Soviet Union to offset U.S. support for Israel. Soviet aid to Egypt included financing of the Aswan High Dam and significant military technical assistance (Sayigh and Shalim, 1997; Laqueur, 1969).

Although Egyptian President Anwar al-Sadat had made overtures to the United States as early as the 1973 war with Israel, the U.S.-Egyptian relationship was significantly transformed by the Egyptian-Israeli peace accords facilitated by the Carter administration at Camp David in 1978. After the signing of the treaty by President al-Sadat and Israeli Prime Minister Menachem Begin in 1979, the United States became the major great-power patron of Egypt and included the Arab nation in its regional alliances. Egypt has since remained a significant ally of the United States. The bonds between the United States and Egypt strengthened further following the fall of the Soviet Union and the end of the Cold War, with Egypt continuing to receive U.S. aid. Egypt cooperated with the United States during the Persian Gulf War of 1991. During this time, U.S. economic interests in, and dependency on, Middle Eastern natural resources became primary drivers of U.S. policy in the region.[1]

The U.S.-Egyptian relationship includes several components, as befits a changing relationship in a volatile region. The most conspicuous has been military aid, including more than $1 billion annually from the United States to Egypt since 1985 (Mark, 2004). Such support was certainly one reason Egypt supported U.S. military actions against Iraq in the early 1990s, including contributing a large deployment of troops (Said Aly and Pelletreau, 2001).

The nations interact in many ways besides military cooperation. Egypt has worked closely with the United States on diplomatic efforts, such as hosting and brokering peace talks between the Israelis and Pal-

---

[1] For further discussion on the need for Arab states to negotiate great-power politics, see Owen (1993).

estinians. Economically, Egypt provides a market for U.S. goods, particularly agricultural foodstuffs. In recent years, Egypt has confronted violent Islamist groups on its own territory and provided crucial support to the U.S. Global War on Terrorism. The United States also engaged the Egyptian government in a dialogue regarding human-rights issues and democratization.

Broadly speaking, U.S.-Egyptian relations have been positive and benefited each state, even through some trying times. Thus, while the two sides have differed at several junctures in the past three decades, the two countries often display a united front in public, as, for example, when Egyptian President Hosni Mubarak met with U.S. President George W. Bush at the latter's Texas ranch in April 2004 (Brinkley and Stevenson, 2004).

However, in its diplomatic endeavors, Egypt has not always acted in the best interests of the United States. Egypt's relations with Libya were considered a liability by the United States until Libya's recent change in policies (Marr, 1999). Egypt also supported a 1997 Arab League resolution calling for an economic boycott of Israel (Satloff, 1997). More recently, while Egypt acquiesced to the transit of U.S. forces engaged in military actions in Iraq, President Mubarak sharply criticized U.S. policy, stating, "Instead of having one [Usama] bin Laden, we will have 100 bin Ladens" ("Mubarak Warns of '100 bin Ladens,'" 2003).

Egypt's opposition to U.S. foreign policy has, at times, led Congress to consider reducing its aid (Said Aly, 2000). The United States has, in fact, reduced economic aid to Egypt, but only to keep it at parity with that provided Israel. Egypt's economic aid is also conditional on the Egyptian government undertaking "significant economic and political reforms" (McConnell, 2005; Mark, 2004).

The history of U.S. economic aid to Egypt is checkered. Prior to the Persian Gulf War of 1991, Egypt had accumulated nearly $50 billion in debt, which was forgiven by the United States after the war (Organisation for Economic Co-operation and Development, 2006; Quandt, 1990). Still, the level of economic aid to Egypt and Egypt's previously high level of debt has led to U.S. pressure on Egypt to make economic reforms. These reforms have at times caused destabilization, as occurred in the 1990s, when Egypt moved to privatize many of its large, state-owned industries at the behest of the International Monetary Fund ("Egypt: Strike over IMF Privatization Policies," 1994). Yet despite its many social and economic problems, including population growth that may be more rapid than its economy can sustain, Egypt remains an important trade partner for the United States, carrying a $1.7 billion trade surplus in 2006. This amount is nearly three times the U.S. economic aid Egypt received that year (Basheer, 1999; Bureau of Economic Analysis, 2007).

The United States has a set of interconnected (and sometimes conflicting) policy objectives in the region. These include reducing the threat of terrorism and pressing for democratic political reform and improvements in human rights. The United States has given Egypt mixed signals in its pursuit of these policies. In 1993, for example, condemnation by the U.S. ambassador of Egyptian human-rights abuses led to official complaints from the Egyptian government (Hedges, 1993). Following terrorist attacks on U.S. embassies in Nairobi, Kenya, and Dar es Salaam, Tanzania, in 1998, President Bill Clinton pointedly mentioned Egypt and its struggle against terrorists in a nationally televised speech but did not mention Egyptian violations of human rights in pursuing terrorists ("Clinton Discusses Military Strikes," 1998).

U.S. support for Egyptian antiterrorism efforts took another turn during George W. Bush's presidency. In his 2003 address to the National Endowment for Democracy, President Bush condemned the authoritarian regimes of the Middle East and suggested Egypt should lead the way toward reform:

> Many Middle Eastern governments now understand that military dictatorship and theocratic rule are a straight, smooth highway to nowhere. But some governments still cling to the old habits of central control. There are governments that still fear and repress independent thought and creativity, and private enterprise—the human qualities that make for a—strong and successful societies. . . . The great and proud nation of Egypt has shown the way toward peace in the Middle East, and now should show the way toward democracy in the Middle East (The White House, 2003).

President Bush also brought up the need for reform when meeting with President Mubarak in April 2004 (The White House, 2004). This brought the issues of human rights and democratization to the forefront of the U.S.-Egyptian relationship. Still, the rhetoric was not supported by a new strategy (Brown and Dunne, 2007). When Egyptian reformers became more vocal during elections in 2005 and were subsequently silenced by a government crackdown, the United States largely declined to chastise the Egyptian regime. Asked about the demonstrations, a spokesman for the U.S. Department of State said,

> So Egypt is a good friend. Egypt is a good ally. We have a lot of common issues that we're working on together in terms—certainly in fighting terrorism, certainly in trying to bring peace to the Middle East. That said, when there are issues that arise like we have seen today, we are going to speak out very plainly about them and that's what friends do. And we're going to be following up with the Egyptian Government on today's events and we would hope that the Egyptian Government would come out and make it very clear that there is support for and the ability to peacefully express views concerning government actions in Egypt (U.S. Department of State, 2006).

Even this mild criticism was tempered when, a month later, President Bush met with Gamal Mubarak, President Mubarak's son and heir apparent (as well as the object of much political rancor in Egypt) and Secretary of State Condoleezza Rice moved to protect aid to Egypt, citing the need to maintain a "strategic partnership" (Stephens, 2006).

Because of this pattern of saying one thing and doing another, there has been some confusion about the real interests of the United States in Egypt, with domestic opponents of the regime frustrated by the lack of concrete U.S. action to promote democratization and the regime reacting with both defensiveness and indifference whenever reform is mentioned (Weisman, 2005). As noted, the United States has a productive relationship with the Egyptian government on several fronts, including in the fight against terrorism. However, in pursuing these interests, it has acquiesced to Egypt's abuse of human rights, particularly in the use of "rendition" to escape the legal requirements imposed by U.S. and international law (Human Rights Watch, 2005a). Consequently, in the area of human rights, the U.S. relationship with Egypt remains somewhat fractious and unpredictable and at any given time is contingent on several considerations, including current domestic politics in both countries, recent incidents of terrorism, and the strategies the United States decides to pursue in the region.

The United States and Egypt share a broad set of goals and interests, finding common ground over the past 15 years in seeking peaceful relations with Israel, regional security, economic development, and the elimination of terrorism. Where common ground has proven elusive, as in the U.S. intervention in Iraq, the Palestinian issue, and democratic reform and human rights within Egypt, they have found ways to disagree without causing a serious rupture in the relationship. Moreover, with respect to democratic reform, as long as an authoritarian regime ensures an Egypt cooperative with U.S. interests, the benefits of a broadly agreeable relationship will significantly lessen the appeal to the United States of a push for significant reform.

Democratization in Egypt During the 1990s

During the 1990s, as the United States was sending mixed signals on democratization, reform, and human rights, Egyptian politics had stagnated. By the dawn of the 21st century, Egyptian democratization had become so stagnant that several observers contended Egypt was less democratic than it had been at any time in the two decades during which President Mubarak had then held office (Ibrahim, 2002; author interviews with journalists and activists, 2006).

To be sure, the Mubarak regime faced several challenges to its authority. In the early 1990s, it was challenged politically by a resurgent Muslim Brotherhood and militarily by even-more-radical Islamists. To thwart the political challenge, the regime relied on an electoral system unfavorable to opposition groups, which in turn caused radicals to boycott subsequent elections (Kassem, 2004). Similarly, after members of the ruling party lost control of the major professional syndicates to the Muslim Brotherhood in 1993, the state changed the rules governing the syndicates, effectively bringing them back under government control (Abdalla, 1993). The regime also cracked down on Islamists, beginning with mass arrests of Muslim Brotherhood members and Islamists belonging to more-radical groups shortly before the elections of 1987 and continuing with mass detentions through the early 1990s (Human Rights Watch, 1993).

During this time, violent confrontations between the government and Islamists in Upper Egypt intensified and spread throughout the country. In response, the regime rounded up vast numbers of suspected Islamists, most of whom were later released (Gerges, 2005). The state also took legislative action against journalists and nongovernmental organizations. A 1995 law expanded restrictions on journalists. A 1999 law allowed the government to dismiss or appoint members to a nongovernmental organization's board of trustees. It also included penalties for organizations that threatened "public morality" or "national unity" (Kassem, 2004, p. 120–121). Parliamentary elections in 1995 clearly indicated a moribund political scene: The opposition garnered little representation in the People's Assembly. In 2000, however, the Supreme Constitutional Court demanded improved supervision of the elections. This resulted in the presence of judges at the polling places, with results characterized as "somewhat cleaner and more credible than the 1990 or 1995 elections" (Dunne, 2006, p. 5). Some observers suggested that these elections showed the regime was in a precarious position. Opposition candidates won only 33 seats in the 444-seat Assembly, but independent candidates captured 218 of the 388 seats attributed to the ruling National Democratic Party. Most of these independents were predisposed toward the National Democratic Party, but the fact that the party's candidates did not win outright was surprising to some analysts (Abdel-Latif, 2000; Al-Anani, 2005b).

Yet liberalization suffered further setbacks with the addition of Articles 75, 76, and 77 to the Egyptian constitution. Article 75 gave the president the power to impose emergency law, Article 76 limited elections to candidates of registered parties (effectively, of the ruling National Democratic Party), and Article 77 permitted the president to remain in office for an unlimited number of terms. Together, these amendments strengthened President Mubarak's hold on the presidency and the National Democratic Party's hold over the Assembly. Anathema to opposition groups, together these articles shook the opposition out of its malaise and reinvigorated it. Among new opposition groups forming in the wake of this turn of events was Kefaya.

Emergence of Kefaya

Though its roots were in earlier reform movements and its impetus was the changes to the Egyptian constitution, the formal beginnings of Kefaya date to late 2004, when hundreds of Egyptian intellectuals gathered to address the issue of executive power. Ahmad Baha' al-Din Sha'ban, one of the principal architects of Kefaya, writes of the event:

> 300 names from among the greatest nationalists and intellectuals in Egypt were gathered. A call was announced for a conference to be held to discuss the next step. The conference was held on September 22, 2004 . . . in which over 500 people were assembled and which concluded with the creation of "The Egyptian Movement for Change" as a flexible framework for the movement that could bring together a wide spectrum of Egyptian nationals of different political affiliations (Sha'ban, 2006, p. 65).

From the onset, Kefaya was not a political party and was not structured as such. Rather, it referred to itself as a "movement." Some Arab intellectuals described it as "an expression of a social phenomenon" (Al-Anani, 2005a). Many believed its nonpolitical status to be "the secret of its beauty since it has been content for citizens—not the authorities, court rooms or discussions behind closed doors—to be the sole judge of its national affiliation" (Al-Anani, 2005a).

In reality, Kefaya was a coalition of political parties united by their demand for a shift in the balance of power. Its slogan (and the name by which it was known), the Arabic word for *enough*, succinctly expressed this sentiment in its demand for President Mubarak to cede power. Although opposition to absolute rule was a major point of coalescence for the organization, the group embraced a number of ambitious goals, the ultimate of which was to break the paralysis of Egyptian politics and discourse and to promote a new political environment more conducive to democratization. In the words of George Ishaq, a cofounder of Kefaya, the organization also more broadly sought to "serve all Egyptians," in contrast to political parties thought to serve only their own interests (author interview, May 2007).

Described as a secular organization, Kefaya was widely diverse, uniting communist, nationalist, and Islamist members in "the most significant model of modern political parties in the Arab world" (Al-Sayied, 2004).[2] This union was historic; there had never been such a coalescence of Egyptian political groups around any set of issues, much less in direct response to the ruler and his potential successor.

Kefaya was unique in calling for regime change. Sha'ban (2006, p. 10) writes,

> Instead of demanding efforts to reform the current regime, the demand became one of completely changing this regime as well as a call for establishing a parliamentary republic in which there would be real separation of power, a judicial system with administrative and financial independence which would not be subservient to the Ministry of Justice, and an elected government which would be accountable to the parliament.

While anti-Mubarak sentiments were not uncommon, Kefaya's anti-Mubarak demonstration was the first ever in Egypt (Howeidy, 2005b).

The principal architects of the Kefaya coalition were as diverse as its political groups. The movement included intellectuals such as Ishaq, its first secretary general (who was a secularist and communist Copt); Majid Ahmad Hussein, an Islamist who ardently believes in the slogan "Islam is the Solution"; and Abul-Ela Madi, an Islamist who founded al-Wasat party, a moderate version of the Muslim Brotherhood. Kefa-

---

[2] Parties and other organizations in the coalition included *al-Wafd* (Delegation), *al-Tajammu*ᶜ (Assembly), *al-Nasiri* (Nasserist), *al-* ᶜ*Amal* (Labor), *al-Karama* (Dignity), *al-Wasat* (Center), and *Jama*ᶜ*at al-Ikhwan al-Muslimin* (Muslim Brotherhood) as well as the National Gathering for Democratic Change, National Coalition for Reform and Change, and Popular Campaign for Change (Egyptian Movement for Change, 2005).

ya's original founders and current leaders have a common history of activism. Most of them have founded or participated in political parties since the 1970s. Many have been jailed for their political views. Almost all of them are well known in the Arabic-language media, where they routinely express their views on various political issues.

Kefaya was at first able to attract members from all segments of Egyptian society. One analyst writes,

> It is not strange to find that its members—as is documented on the movement's website (www.harakamasria.com)—include many low-level professionals (plumbers, carpenters, launderers, etc.) as well as their middle-class counterparts (journalists, researchers, students, businessmen, accountants, university professors, doctors, professionals, artists, etc.). It also includes members from upper-class groups such as politicians and bank employees (Al-Anani, 2005a).

Importantly, Kefaya's diversity reflected longstanding political trends in Egypt: the leftist and Islamist. The cross-cutting ideological orientation of Kefaya was actually part of a broader cooperation between differing factions that has been a feature of Egyptian politics for decades. The involvement of some Kefaya members in political activism dated to the 1970s student movement in Egypt. Activists who later became the core of Kefaya's leadership were profoundly influenced by the key phases of the student movement and by the critical junctures or events that shaped its politics. While the period surrounding the wars of 1967 and 1973 saw Arab nationalism reach a nadir and the concomitant rise of Islamist movements amid a sobering economic climate in Egypt, it also saw consensus form around one key issue—foreign policy. While divergent in ideology, many groups were united in their opposition to Israel. Members also observed the suppression of leftist movements, the rise of Islamist organizations, and, ultimately, ideological fragmentation that allowed a permissive environment for state control of all opposition, all of which served to create resistance to authoritarian rule in Egypt in addition to the initial focus of the movement—opposition to Israel (and later, criticism of the U.S. approach to the conflict). Members of this 1970s student cohort continued to meet well into the 1990s in an effort to formulate proposals and statements on those issues that transcended their ideological differences (Shorbagy, 2007).

Kefaya's leaders took their agenda to the Arab media. On Al-Jazeera television, Iman Ramadan, one of Kefaya's founders, advocated doing away with the Emergency Laws in place since the beginning of the Mubarak regime, as well as other laws that restrict liberties. He also suggested limiting a president to two six-year terms, curtailing the absolute authority of the executive, a separation of powers, increasing the freedom to establish parties and freedom of the press, lifting the restrictions on forming unions, and holding open parliamentary elections under complete judicial supervision ("The Internal Crisis Within the Egyptian Kefaya Movement," 2006).

Kefaya's initial focus was domestic. Many of its leaders divorced themselves from the rallying around external causes that had been heavily encouraged by the regime, causes such as attacking U.S. foreign policy or supporting Palestinians and Iraqis. They argued,

> It makes no sense at all for us to have nearly 20 committees and organizations for standing in solidarity with the Palestinian and Iraqi peoples while there is no more than one or two small committees for being in solidarity with the Egyptian people and their causes. It is not logical for dozens of conferences, seminars, lectures, etc. to be organized on an annual basis for standing in solidarity with our brothers and sisters in Palestine and Iraq while no efforts worth mentioning are organized to be in solidarity with farmers who suffer under new and unjust laws formulated to strip them of their land, workers who are fired from their factories, the millions of youth who are unemployed, the thousands who are imprisoned and detained, the hundreds who are tortured in police stations, or those who suffer from rising prices, inflation, economic stagnation, etc.! (Sha'ban, 2006, p. 45)

Kefaya's leadership would eventually be forced to defend this focus by arguing it could best support victimized Arab brothers by starting with internal reform. They suggested, "Egypt ruled by tyranny and backwardness—in which corruption is prevalent—cannot offer anything worth mentioning, especially for the Palestinians" (Sha'ban, 2006, p. 11).

Kefaya was soon recognized as "more popular and effective than all other and much older ideological, nationalist, and leftist movements" (Caten, 2005). One journalist wrote,

> Beyond any doubt, the emergence of Kefaya can be considered a clear condemnation of the political performance of Egyptian parties. That is, if the latter had been able to bridge the gap . . . neither "Kefaya" nor any other party would have had any legitimacy as a political alternative for the organizational frameworks which now exist—especially since the basic spectrum of "Kefaya" is made up of members, leaders, and activists from the existing political parties as well as independent political forces and members of the general public who lack partisan or organizational experience (Al-Sultan, 2005).

Consistent with its claim to represent all Egyptians, the group advocated on behalf of Egyptian victims of the Red Sea ferry accident of 2006, launched protests denouncing the infamous Danish caricatures of the Prophet Mohammed, and organized a march in commemoration of International Students' Day.

Eventually, as we will discuss, partisanship would divide the movement. Nevertheless, at its founding, Kefaya represented a growing awareness within Arab intellectual and business circles that many pressing issues—including the protection of civil liberties, limited intellectual development, declining indicators of growth, high and growing levels of poverty, the incompatibility of social and economic structures in the Arab world with those in the West, and corruption—were not being properly addressed (Sha'ban, 2006).

According to Kefaya member Mustafa Kamil Al Sayid, the peaceful, grassroots democratization movements of Eastern Europe and Central Asia—particularly Georgia's Revolution of the Roses, which led to the collapse of Eduard Shevardnadze's regime, and Ukraine's Orange Revolution—were particularly inspirational and instructive for Kefaya (author interview, May 2007). These were peaceful mass movements that produced political change.

The momentum that Kefaya enjoyed at its inception encouraged Kefaya leaders. As foreign movements had influenced them, so they hoped to spark similar organizations in other countries in the Middle East. They spoke extensively of the "butterfly" or "ripple" effect that they hoped their movement would have. Describing how this effect might emerge from an initial event, Sha'ban (2006, p. 13) writes,

> This event itself might be simple and slight, but it generates a series of consecutive results and successive developments that gradually increase in size to far exceed the initial event. These occur in ways, locations and times that are completely unexpected and unpredictable.

There were many aspects of the Kefaya movement that were unexpectedly successful, particularly given the Mubarak regime's past success in silencing opposition movements. In the next chapter, we will review some of the successes Kefaya enjoyed. There were also many challenges that Kefaya faced, and our discussion of its achievements will be followed by a review of the problems it encountered, many of which are not unique to Kefaya and are faced by other reform movements in the region.

CHAPTER THREE

Kefaya's Successes

The initial demonstrations held by Kefaya, with their message of "No to a fifth term and no to hereditary rule" and their implicit challenge to a sitting regime, was, as noted, unprecedented in Egyptian politics (El-Din, 2004). This direct challenge to a sitting ruler earned Kefaya praise from both the Arab and international presses.

Many intellectuals viewed Kefaya as an example of what an Egyptian political party should be. One observer wrote,

> In its activities, Kefaya relies on openness, transparency and using peaceful means. It is democratic in its internal relations and is therefore different from the ideological parties which rely on their members being subjected to a hierarchical system (Caten, 2005).

Kefaya's own architects were surprised by the public reception of the movement and its ability to mobilize diverse communities, especially given that it did not have the Muslim Brotherhood's financial network, the Mubarak regime's media platforms, or the legacy that many older parties enjoyed (Sha'ban, 2006).

What lay behind Kefaya's successful emergence? How did it use this success? We address these questions below, exploring Kefaya's message, its ability to form peaceful coalitions in opposition to the regime, and its use of information technology.

Timing and Simplicity of Message

Kefaya developed simple but potent slogans that captured the imagination of its followers and were more effective than those of more-complicated initiatives. Its very name, *Enough!*, resonated very well among the masses and elite. Its message of "*la lil-tawrith, la lil-tamdid*" ["No to inheritance, no to extension"] crystallized the issue of hereditary rule for Egyptians (Al-Shubki, 2007). One observer attributed Kefaya's comparative success to its "simple analysis of the situation which any citizen is able to understand" (Caten, 2005).

Position to Mobilize and Form Coalitions

From its birth, Kefaya was based on coalition building and uniting otherwise conflicting parties in support of broadly acceptable democratic political reforms. While Kefaya's coalition eventually splintered, its capacity to build such alliances in the first place is outstanding. For a time, the movement was able to attract disparate parts of Egypt's opposition. Kefaya also reached out to reform-minded individuals from a wide spectrum of social and professional status. At its peak, the organization was present in 24 of 26 provinces throughout Egypt and, during the initial phase of its founding, held protests with thousands of members (author interview with a former senior Kefaya member, May 2007). It created a group called Youth for Change that "addressed the new generations in appropriate ways," such as via the Internet and music, and "linked the Egyptian street with the masses all over the country" (Sha'ban, 2006, p. 135). Although some youth were afraid of being arrested, their frustration helped to overcome this fear.[1] As one youth said at a Kefaya meeting, "Of course, I am afraid, but there is nothing else for me to do. I have no life, no job, and no future" (Sharib, 2005). Another commented, "In any other country, students are the force behind political change. But here we have no

---

[1] This frustration is not unfounded; more than 90 percent of Egypt's unemployed are between 15 and 25 years old (International Labour Organization, 2006).

role" (Sharib, 2005). Kefaya granted a role to the youth, and many exploited this opportunity.

The movement's mobilization also included almost every major profession in Egypt. Sha'ban (2006, p. 70) writes,

> The call spread within Egyptian society—horizontally, vertically and within a record period of time. Formal versions of the movement were created in numerous sectors: Professors for Change, Youth for Change, Engineers for Change, Journalists for Change, Authors and Artists for Change. All these groups called for democratic change within society in keeping with demands within their field of specialty.

Kefaya also mobilized farmers, judges, and even children. Judges formed an alliance to lead calls for legal reform and for oversight of the elections without interference from the government and its security forces (Al-Aryan, 2007). Kefaya staged a demonstration by children in support of an estimated 30,000 political detainees, highlighting the stories of children who had not seen their relatives for years, including some children whose relatives had been imprisoned without receiving trial from the time of their birth (Howeidy, 2005b).

Perhaps one reason for Kefaya's ability to mobilize wide segments of society was its use of popular icons of Egyptian culture (Hassan, 2005). Ahmad Fu'ad Najam, a legendary dissident in Egypt, recited his popular poems during conferences and protests. Famous actors marched in demonstrations alongside other protestors.

Setting an Example of Peaceful Opposition

At a time when the Middle East has been ravaged by extremism, with its calls for jihadist violence to bring change, Kefaya set an example of peaceful activism. Kefaya's leaders spoke out against violence and prided themselves on "reviving the legitimacy of peaceful democratic struggle after it has gradually been confiscated over the course of more than 50 years . . . and violence of radical Islamic organizations has come to seem the only way" (Sha'ban, 2006, p. 11). When Ayman al-Zawahiri, a native of Egypt and prominent leader of al-Qaeda, condemned Kefaya's peaceful approach, asserting that "the only way to confront tyrannical rulers and the crusader forces is through *jihad*." Kefaya responded by declaring that "peaceful democratic transformation is the sole way for Egypt to get out of its comprehensive crisis" and that it "openly condemned and completely rejected cowardly terrorist operations" (Sha'ban, 2006, p. 17; "The Kefaya Movement Condemns Terrorism," 2005).

In addition to holding peaceful protests, Kefaya organized candlelight vigils and evening chanting events (Abd Al-Llah, 2005). It sought to be humorous in making its case, as in one protest in which participants carried brooms, symbolizing the need to "clean up" Egyptian politics.

Aspiring to establish the rule of law at every level in the Egyptian government, Kefaya looked to the West for models. Its Web site noted,

> There is no doubt that the democratic environment these countries enjoy has led to accountability where no official, even the president himself, is above the law. Rather, he is held accountable and even punished if found guilty. In these countries, the media enjoys credibility, as they are not under pressure. They are able to expose corruption and scandals such as the Lewinsky case which occurred in the United States ("The Corruption File," 2006).

Indeed, according to some accounts, Kefaya was inspired by "peaceful civil revolutions in the West that led to political change, namely the Orange Revolution in Ukraine" (Khalil, 2005).

Successful Exploitation of Information Technology

Kefaya successfully exploited information technology. It allowed unconditional membership in its organization and on its Web site. Members were able to anonymously "post their grievances online" (Caten, 2005).

Kefaya used four primary means of communications. First, it contacted its members and the general public using electronic messages. Second, it published advertisements online and in independent media outlets, if possible. Third, it published banners and caricatures (political cartoons) on its own Web site and on those of supporting bloggers. Fourth, it gathered audiovisual and photographic documentation of sexual and physical harassment by state security officers.

Egyptian antiwar demonstrations in 2003 were advertised through email and text messages (Schemm, 2003). Kefaya adopted the same approach to safely communicate with the general public. For example, a text message sent to thousands of mobile phones helped draw 2,000 persons to a June 2005 demonstration that one report described as "the most organized and impressive demonstration by the reform movement to date" (Howeidy, 2005a). Kefaya advertised events in its online calendar, sent text messages to as many mobile phones as possible, emailed original members regularly, and called for support from bloggers.

It was much easier for Kefaya to advertise via electronic means than in newspapers, which were likely to have been censored by the government. For example, Kefaya was able to advertise a September 2007 rally in support of freedom of the press on the *Wehda Masrya* [Egyptian Unity] blog, but saw all copies of the independent newspaper *Al-Karama* [*Dignity*] confiscated when it advertised an anti-Mubarak rally in it (Wehda Masrya, 2007; Zaki, 2007b).

Several bloggers carried banners calling for a prohibition against hereditary rule, the release of Kefaya activists, and the enforcement of antitorture laws. A banner displaying Gamal Mubarak's photograph read, "The National Initiative Against Hereditary Rule." Other banners called for the release of Ayman Nour, a presidential candidate who challenged Mubarak (and was not a Kefaya member), and of Kareem Amer, a blogger jailed for defaming President Mubarak and criticizing Islam. Kefaya's Web site carried antitorture banners and caricatures. Another common caricature showed a police officer carrying the Egyptian currency as a national flag and depicted other government officials as mobsters and corrupt employees (Abbas, 2007).

Blogs and other new media also documented physical and sexual abuse committed by state police. In one posted video, a uniformed officer slaps a detainee who tried to protect his face (Abbas, 2007). A YouTube video showed a prisoner being sodomized with a stick while being mocked by the officers around him (Hairman180, 2006). A blogger posted pictures of the officers involved under a "Wanted" heading (El Masri, 2007). On its own Web site, Kefaya published an article denouncing torture by state security and announcing the creation of Egyptians Against Torture to document cases of torture and provide support to victims ("Egyptians Against Torture," 2007). Such documentation has helped draw international attention to the Egyptian government's human-rights abuses (Pannell, 2007).

Kefaya's Internet Strategy

Kefaya's Internet strategy focused first on bloggers, second on the general public, and third on local and international media. The flow of information between these elements increased the chances of accomplishing a specific outcome (Howeidy, 2005a; "US State Secretary Cancels Trip to Egypt," 2005; Abbas, 2005).

Kefaya had three domains of action: an inner circle of activists, a coordinator, and a spokesperson (Shorbagy, 2007). For its Web-based activities, Kefaya relied on the inner circle of activists to maintain a continual flow of ideas and to encourage others to speak out. These activists maintained a forum for debate on Kefaya's Web site where interested parties from the general public could voice their opinions on government corruption, the performance of Egyptian embassies around the world, the Muslim Brotherhood, and other topics. They could use the forum to document corruption and police brutality, monitor local events, and publish articles. As noted, blogs have been closely linked to the emergence of the Kefaya movement, with many activists using this technology (Al-Malky, 2007). Nevertheless, in a nation with only six million Internet users (Central Intelligence Agency, 2008), there are limits to the effectiveness of Internet strategies that will only reach about 7 percent of the population.

Bloggers

Bloggers provided Kefaya with one means to mobilize. Many bloggers adhere to the same political message as did Kefaya, opposing a fifth term for President Mubarak and his succession by his son. Many also seek genuine democratic reforms. In addition to its own insignia (a yellow circle containing *Kefaya* written in red), the banners of bloggers could often be seen on Kefaya's Web site. Kefaya's insignia could also be seen online outside if its own Web site, for example on blogs such as wa7damasrya.blogspot.com and misrdigital.blogspirit.com. Bloggers also augmented Kefaya's efforts to document human-rights abuses, including, in addition to the sodomization of a prisoner by a police officer noted above, sexual assaults on women in downtown Cairo during Ramadan and the trial of Kareem Nabil, who was sentenced to three years in prison for insulting Islam and inciting riot (Al-Malky, 2007; "Campaign to Free the Brave Egyptian Blogger Abdulkareem nabil Soliman," 2007). Summarizing the ways bloggers augment Kefaya's efforts, one analyst writes,

> If Kefaya has provided the political space for voices of opposition to speak out, blogs have provided the means for Kefaya's mobilization. Not only have the bloggers continued to challenge the official version of events—exposing a wide array of abuses by Egypt's authorities and monitoring the lives of fellow activists in jail—they have also rallied other activists around the cause of publicizing Kefaya demonstrations which have often been overlooked by mainstream publications (Al-Malky, 2007, p. 4).

General Public

Kefaya relied extensively on the general public to propagate its message and join its demonstrations and activities. It accepted persons of all political and religious affiliations, including Marxists, atheists, Islamists, Liberals, and Nasserites, because its goal is simple and accepted by all opposition parties. Bloggers also encouraged the public to participate in Kefaya's events (see, for example, Zaki, 2007a, a blog post encouraging attendance at a March 2007 protest of government restrictions on freedom and human rights). Bloggers acknowledged that Kefaya knew the importance of attracting persons to upcoming demonstrations and therefore continued to advertise them (Mohamed from Cairo, 2005).

Media

Kefaya also sought to influence international and independent media to pressure the regime. Kefaya-documented abuses of human rights have been reported by Al-Jazeera, the BBC, the *Washington Post*, the *New York Times*, CNN, and nongovernmental organizations such as Human Rights Watch and Amnesty International. In some cases, independent newspapers in Egypt (such as *Al-Karama*) have reprinted posts written by bloggers without even editing them (Al-Malky, 2007). The state's violent reaction to demonstrations in 2005 led U.S. Secretary of State Condoleezza Rice to cancel a visit to Egypt. One of Kefaya's founders, Abu el-Maadi, claimed international pressure on Mubarak "has helped to curb government repression" by allowing protestors to gather without being assaulted (Shadid, 2007).

Challenging the Regime

Kefaya leaders see their greatest accomplishment as the breaking down of obstacles to direct confrontation of regime policies. Previous to the Kefaya movement, activists never dared to say "no" directly to the symbols of power, President Mubarak and his son, for fear of repression. As one journalist writes,

> No one could get anywhere near the President. No one could talk about the prolongation of the presidency as if he were a Pharaoh who lives and possesses the throne forever. The Kefaya movement had the audacity and bravery to pull the Pharaoh down from his sacred untouchable status to one within the human sphere where we could say to him: "No. No, we do not want you forever. We do not want your son. We do not want a hereditary throne." This bold action from Kefaya is enough of an accomplishment all by itself ("The Internal Crisis Within the Egyptian Kefaya Movement," 2006).

Inspiration for Others: Kefaya's National and International Influence

Kefaya's successes have inspired similar movements in Egypt and abroad. Within Egypt, Kefaya is credited with inspiring labor protests. One journalist recently observed that

> Throughout the last 60 years, Egypt has not known the likes of the wave of labor strikes that have shaken it in recent months. In 2006 alone, more than 600 labor strikes have taken place. The tension of the strikes has become amplified with the deterioration of living and economic conditions (Yahya, 2007).

These protests were independent of Kefaya but inspired by it. As one columnist claimed, Kefaya may have been the "heart of reform movements." Perhaps Kefaya's greatest significance was in serving as a catalyst for all those wishing to protest the current situation. Kefaya planted the seeds of protest, an act that had been taboo previously (Yahya, 2007).

Kefaya similarly inspired protests elsewhere that had been taboo previously. In Libya, Khalas, whose name is another Arabic word for *enough*, formed to oppose Colonel Muammar al-Qaddafi's retention of power ("Benefits from the Experience of the Kefaya Movement of Egypt," 2005). Similarly inspired by Kefaya, the Sudan Platform gathered 3,000 Sudanese to oppose the government of Omar al-Bashir ("In the Same Mode as the Egypt Movement," 2006). In still other parts of the world, there have been protests undertaken in solidarity with Kefaya ("Kefaya Accuses the Police of Ravishing the Honor of One of Its Activists," 2006).

CHAPTER FOUR

Kefaya's Decline

For some time after its creation, journalists marveled at Kefaya's ability to withstand "ferocious attacks from the state" (El-Anani, 2005). Eventually, however, Kefaya succumbed to these blows and its successes for the most part withered away.

The political and social dynamics that led to Kefaya's decline can be grouped into four general categories: first, Kefaya's struggle against the state over the misuse of power, the manipulation of laws, and the control of the media; second, Kefaya's relationship with Islamists; third, the role of the ruling elite in propagating antidemocratic messages; and fourth, Kefaya's own internal organizational problems.

The general causes of Kefaya's decline are not unique. Rather, they are the same that challenge the spread of democracy throughout the Arab world. Shedding light on these obstacles can offer insights as to how these barriers hinder democratic initiatives throughout the region, and, perhaps, how they may be overcome.

Intimidation by the State

Authoritarian regimes in the Arab world have a significant capacity to effect change within the societies they govern. State repression is the main cause of political stagnation. The Mubarak regime used its capacity to manipulate laws and deploy security forces to ultimately render Kefaya impotent. Indeed, one analyst suggested that the Egyptian government's mastery in evading democracy is so brilliant that "it should be studied" (Hasan, 2007).

When nonviolent techniques such as co-option and division are not effective, the Mubarak regime resorts to violent repression. Activists who responded to Kefaya's calls encountered an overwhelming number of security agents. Many of these protesters were beaten and detained without charges or trials, as the state has the power to do. Most of those detained were tortured, a fairly common practice in Egyptian prisons. Those who were not detained were still subjected to physical abuse. The assault of protestors by security officers and soldiers dressed in civilian clothes became routine at Kefaya demonstrations ("Detainment of Kefaya Leaders and Members," 2005). A typical report of a Kefaya demonstration noted, "The scene repeated itself yet again as the Kefaya movement hit the streets. The police surround the protestors in every instance" ("The Kefaya Movement—Challenges and Factions," 2006).

State aggression against Kefaya also included sexual harassment and the rape of women in public places to intimidate women from participating in protests. Egyptian journalists condemned these acts, especially when one of the women raped in public was a journalist ("83% Voted in Favor of Amending the Constitution," 2005). Foreign news agencies reported these abuses, with some reports including photographs or videos of the security forces molesting women and tearing off their clothes in public (see, for example, "What Happened in Cairo?" 2005).

One of the most notorious attacks against a journalist targeted Abd al-Halim Qandil, editor-in-chief of the opposition Nasserist newspaper *al-Arabi* [*The Arab*] and a prominent Kefaya leader ("The Events of Several Months of Assaults on Members of the Media," 2005). Within 48 hours of writing about Gamal Mubarak's imminent inheritance of the presidency and the continuation of the decades-long state of emergency, he was kidnapped in front of his house, stripped of his clothes, beaten, and then flung into the desert.

Kefaya condemned these attacks, its leaders demanding the "rapid release of these protestors as their detention violates the Egyptian constitution and international conventions pertaining to human rights" ("The Egyptian Organization Demands the Immediate Release of Protestors of the Kefaya Movement," 2005). Surprisingly, the Egyptian

National Human Rights Institute, created under pressure from the United States but often viewed as close to the regime, also reported these abuses of human rights, detailing the state's abuse of rights in Egyptian prisons, including deaths resulting from torture (Cardenas and Flibbert, 2005).

The state also sent threats to Kefaya leaders warning them against staging protests. Kefaya's general secretary said that he received "strong warnings" against demonstrations, noting, "The security was not content to simply surround, but bared its fangs and dealt with things in an extremely rough manner" ("Why Has Its Popularity Declined?" 2007). These tactics eventually led to a decrease in the number of (and attendance at) Kefaya protests.

Kefaya sought to bring state tactics against it to public attention. The state in turn allegedly targeted Kefaya's boosters. The popular actor Abdel Aziz Makhyoun, a secular member of the leftist Assembly Party, founder of the Green Party of Egypt, and sympathizer with the Muslim Brotherhood, claimed his affiliation with Kefaya caused him to be the target of an assassination attempt and his house to be bugged and wiretapped (Ismael, 2005).

International organizations documented state attacks on Kefaya demonstrators. A Human Rights Watch report noted,

> Security men wearing civilian clothes struck the protestors in Cairo. The anti-riot police permitted these mobs, who were Mubarak supporters, to beat protestors and journalists and physically assault them. In fact, they even encouraged them to do so at times (Human Rights Watch, 2005b).

Amnesty International expressed "serious concern" over the continuous arrest of government critics and demonstrators (Tackaberry, 2005). Solidaire sans Frontieres [Solidarity Without Borders] reported human-rights violations of the Egyptian regime and published a petition circulated by opposition leaders with more than 200 signatures calling on the Egyptian government to end military trials of civilians and criminalization of political dissent, a result of the Emergency Law that has been in place since 1981 (Solidaire sans Frontieres, 2007). The United Nations also expressed "grave concern over recent attacks against the judicial system in Egypt" (Office of the United Nations High Commissioner for Human Rights, 2006). The United Nations expressed alarm regarding the severe repression of demonstrations organized by activists in support of the judicial system. As a result of Kefaya's activism, it urged the Egyptian government to guarantee freedoms and independence of the judicial system.

Still, there was little action in Egypt or abroad to stop the state's abuse of Kefaya. Kefaya members became less willing to subject themselves to state cruelty and eventually were intimidated to the point where they would no longer participate in protests.

Manipulation of "Reform" Laws

In response to Kefaya's pressure, the government passed some "reform amendments" to the constitution. Nevertheless, it quickly became evident that the amendments served to cement the ruling party's grip on power. For example, an amendment to the Emergency Law gave "security authorities absolute power to violate personal liberties without imposing a state of emergency" (Al-Aryan, 2007). One activist described the manipulation of the law by noting,

> It could be said that this is against terrorists. We will refer at this point to the definition of "terrorism" as stipulated by Article 86B of the Law of Penalties which widens the definition into a very flexible framework which makes even an infringement on the general system or intimidation an "act of terrorism." This makes all demonstrators, journalists, politicians, and those who are in opposition subject to punishment under the law as well as movements for which legitimacy has been withdrawn (Al-Aryan, 2007).

Such nominal reforms are common in the Arab world and have led to a separation between regimes and peoples. As one analyst writes,

> There is a state of immense hatred between the rulers in the Arab world and the Arab populace who want these governments to dis-

> appear and lose their thrones that are simply based on corruption and systematic stealing [of] the wealth of the homeland. The governments have responded by indulging themselves in even more corruption and repression of the people, using a bunch of laws that institutionalize their grip on power (El-Zohery, 2006).

Article 76 was amended to allow multiple candidates to run for president, but this new law made it virtually impossible for any candidate to run without the approval of the ruling party (Al-Aryan, 2007). Kefaya considered the amendment an "embellishment of the laws of the ruling party which are in reality dedicated to authority remaining in the hands of the president and paving the way for his son to succeed him" ("83% Voted in Favor of Amending the Constitution," 2005). The International Crisis Group described the multi-candidate presidential elections as a "false start for reform" aiming to "distract attention from the need for deeper political reform" (International Crisis Group, 2005).

Many believe the so-called reforms were never intended to placate the Egyptian public. Indeed, one intellectual argues that Middle Easterners are fully aware that "what these regimes have mentioned regarding reforms and democracy is simply meaningless propaganda directed at a foreign audience" and that the regimes have made clear that democracy and civil rights will not be offered to the people (BilQzeez, 2007, p. 13).

State-Controlled Media

In a country where the government controls most of the media outlets, the state has complete autonomy to vilify its opponents, portray them as traitors, or dismiss them altogether. Leading Egyptian newspapers gave a platform to elites who periodically accused Kefaya of "carrying out U.S. orders and serving a U.S. plan to rock the country's stability" (Sha'ban, 2006, p. 154). In other instances, Kefaya was ridiculed and dismissed as having goals that were "closer to daydreams" (Al-Shubki, 2007). A Media Watch report found that, during the election campaign, the media, particularly government-owned daily newspapers, tended to be biased in favor of the ruling National Democratic Party (Al-Misri, 2005).

Government officials also sought to attack Kefaya in international media. Mubarak himself expressed "strong criticism" of Kefaya to *Le Figaro*, accusing the movement of exploiting international conditions to put pressure on the regime and gain strength from abroad and expressing suspicions about its sources of funding ("Is the Kefaya Movement Changing into a Party?" 2004). Rumors circulated that Kefaya obtained funding from the U.S. Central Intelligence Agency. Kefaya, lacking access to media the state had, was clearly at a disadvantage in responding to such defamation.

The Faltering of the Coalition with the Islamists

At first, Kefaya was able to negotiate and work with some Islamists. Later, this alliance would crumble, as some Islamists withdrew from Kefaya because of the alleged marginalization of the Muslim Brotherhood and the Islamist Labor Party (Ismael, 2006). An Islamist Kefaya leader accused the secularists of attempting to monopolize the movement ("The Internal Crisis Within the Egyptian Kefaya Movement," 2006). At the same time, the movement's secular followers claimed that it had been taken over by Islamists, especially after its new Islamist secretary-general attacked secularism on Al-Jazeera (Youssef, 2007).

One particular issue of contention between Islamists and secularists was Kefaya declining to take an anti-American and anti-Israel stance. This led to the withdrawal of Youth for Change from the coalition, which claimed, "The most critical issue, which is the U.S.-Zionist aggression, was marginalized in the movement's charter. This has given the masses who observe the activities of the movement a bad impression" ("The Labor Party and Youth for Change Withdraw from Kefaya," 2006). Islamists were also alienated when Kefaya's first secretary-general, George Ishaq, attended U.S. conferences alongside Israelis ("The Internal Crisis Within the Kefaya Movement," 2006). When Islamists were able to weigh in and hold protests opposing the U.S. occupation of Iraq and the Israeli occupation of Palestine, many secularists in the movement believed that these protests were exploited by the regime to eradicate Western support for the movement, further alienating secular members who wanted the movement to focus on internal issues (Khalil, 2005).

Another issue that caused the coalition to falter was the inability of the various Kefaya leaders to overcome some ideological differences. For example, the issue of *hijab* [veil] caused tension when the Minister of Culture made a statement against wearing the *hijab* and some secular members of Kefaya supported the Minister's stance. Islamists were outraged, claiming "all activities within the movement itself should be carried to defend Islam against [such] attacks" and that those who issued the anti-*hijab* statements are "not simply against the Brotherhood or Islamists, but against the entire Islamic nation" (Ismael, 2006). Seven senior leaders of Kefaya withdrew as a result of the *hijab* issue (El-Sayed, 2006).

Underlying the *hijab* dispute were differing conceptions of democracy. Tarabishi (1998, p. 17) writes,

> Arab societies want to apply political democracy but not societal democracy. They reject a democracy that gives, for example, equal rights to men and women, sexual freedoms to women, or freedom for homosexuals.

Yet a society cannot be fully democratic if it deprives certain groups of its citizens of their rights. Both secularists and Islamists seem to be at odds as to how far their understanding of democracy goes. Secularists have been accused of being ambivalent (if not hostile) to the religious freedoms of the Islamists and their right to enjoy representation. At the same time, many claim the Islamists "are unable to grasp or comprehend what democracy entails as a philosophy of human value since it advocates liberty and breaking down the barriers which obstruct individual creativity" and that they continually and mistakenly equate the free human being with the depraved human being, considering Western freedom to be synonymous with depravity and immorality (Al-Kuwari, 2004, p. 42).

Kefaya secularists feared what the Islamists might do if they were to win power through democracy. Tarabishi (1998, p. 15) writes,

> It is true that some marginal groups within the radical Islamic movement emphasize democratic values as a slogan, but the majority of them publicly avoid democracy. As the name indicates, it is a western idea within a culture where western civilization as a whole is rejected. Even if radical Islamic groups gain authority through democratic means, the first thing they are likely to do is to ban democracy as a practice, mainly because it is an imported and foreign system. This notion was made public by the second in command within the Algerian Islamic Salvation Front. This brings up a fourth crisis for Arab democracies: should freedom to exercise political activities be granted to political powers that do not believe in democracy and only use it as means and not as a best practice to strive for?

When the Muslim Brotherhood made significant gains in the parliamentary elections, "moderate and enlightened groups as well as Copts in particular . . . received the news of the elections with great distress" (Sha'ban, 2006, p. 97). Such groups strongly oppose a religious state. Their position was that "a state should not have a say in moral beliefs or religious matters [but] should guarantee that its citizens can practice any belief of their own choice" (Tarabishi, 1998, p. 46). Islamists have not taken a unified stance on guaranteeing freedom for others who do not share their degree of faith, even when they share the same religion.

Kefaya was faced with an inability to reconcile differences between different ideological threads and negotiate a united stance, a skill required for successful democratic participation. The challenge of accommodating both secular and religious opposition organizations is prevalent throughout the region as it struggles with issues such as the relationship between politics and religion and combining secular education with institutions of religious education ("The Role of Scholars and the Issue of Legacy of the Prophets," 2006). Kefaya members could have dealt with this challenge more wisely had they focused on their complementary traits. For example, while secularists bring international respectability and connections, Islamists are considered by more Egyptians to be more trustworthy and authentic. Hence, Islamists have a larger number of followers. The fear and suspicion the secularists and Islamists felt for one another undermined what was a fruitful partnership built on mutual anticorruption and anti-authoritarian goals.

Authoritarian governments may seek to exacerbate this divide. The Egyptian government in particular has exploited the mistrust between secularists and Islamists, "playing one side against the other so as to destroy them both and thwart the potential for democratic change" (Gerges, 2004, p. 29). Arab regimes clearly have to address the grievances of the Islamic public, as the use of security forces to suppress groups airing grievances by force and intimidation has essentially failed to destroy these groups and may have actually exacerbated the problem.

Problems with the Elite and the Antidemocracy Message

The Arab world has few experiences with or memories of democracy. Its very meaning is the object of speculation, debate, and conflicting interpretations. The ruling elites who monopolize power view democracy as a threat to their survival and consequently promote antidemocratic messages. Arab intellectuals who promote democracy are treated as political dissidents and punished as such. Kefaya's biggest challenge in fomenting democracy may therefore be analogous to attempting to plant a seedling in sandy soil where it cannot take root or grow.

Kefaya's failure to bring about democratic reform reflects the overall failure of political and intellectual elites who, Al-Sayied (2004, p. 79) claims, share initial "responsibility for institutionalizing totalitarianism." Yet even today, this class cannot agree amongst themselves how and where best to implement democracy.

Nawal al-Sa'dawi (2007), a leading Egyptian writer and feminist, believes that the interests of the ruling elite are inextricably linked to "religion, power, and money," as well as maintaining the status quo, making it very difficult for them to bring about any real change. Al-Sa'dawi believes that those who call for greater freedom for the religious parties are actually in alignment with the ruling elites fighting change. Al-Sa'dawi argues that they are not calling for freedom for all sectors of society but only for the religious parties that reject democratic reform and stand against greater political freedom for those who differ from them ideologically, such as secularists.

Gerges similarly claims the ruling elites exploit various rationales, such as national security, to thwart democracy. Two particular, interlinked issues that are exploited are Zionism and U.S. interests in the region, the subject of much rhetoric from Middle Eastern officials. Arab rulers claim instituting democratic practices might "limit the ability of Arab countries to respond to external challenges, especially those from U.S. and Zionist conspiracies and hegemony" (Gerges, 2004, p. 25).

Rather than educating the masses about democracy, the ruling elite "devote far greater attention to U.S. foreign policy than to domestic politics and society." This enables the regime to deflect attention from principal issues of reform.

The press mirrors this obsession with U.S. foreign policy. One analysis found that

> dozens of opinion pieces and editorials dealing with foreign policy have emphasized the utter disregard by the United States for the sovereignty of small states, international norms and conventions, the aggressive and imperialist nature of its foreign policy, the disproportionate role of Neoconservatives and Zionists in its composition and the obsession (post-9/11) with fighting Islamic terrorism above all else (Baroudi, 2007).

Our own survey of prominent media confirms this finding. Articles criticizing U.S. foreign policy take the lion's share of opinion articles. Articles critical of internal issues are rarely published. This can perhaps be attributed to government control of most media outlets in the Arab world.

Anti-U.S. rhetoric is, of course, a problem beyond Egypt. Moreover, the unpopularity of U.S. foreign policy in the region arises not only because it is highlighted by rulers as a way to distract the public from internal issues: It is likely that many American policies would be perceived as against the interests of Arabs and Muslims regardless of media ownership and reporting. Nevertheless, attacks on U.S. policies create a problem when the United States wishes to support democracy and human rights anywhere in the Middle East. One way that the United States might combat its negative image in the Middle East is to expose more Arabs to U.S. life and culture, perhaps permitting more Arabs to visit and study in the United States.

Antidemocratic messages and messengers generally enjoy government support. Such messengers warn that democracy "bears great threats and dangers" for their society, "threatens the unity and stability of countries," and "does not necessarily assist economic and social progress"; they also argue that "enlightened absolute rule can realize excellent rates of economic growth" (Tarabishi, 1998). As one author explains,

> Democracy does not work in our countries for several reasons. It does not correspond with the development of our societies. It does not suit the culture prevalent within them. It damages them and weakens their national composition. It is not appropriate for the religious and ethnic diversity in our societies. It has no chance of success (Al-Kuwari, 2004, p. 171).

To overcome resistance to democracy, Tarabishi (1998, p. 13) suggests first educating the masses about democracy, arguing,

> Since dictatorships and sectarian politics alternate power in a consecutive fashion, the Arab world does not need to abruptly overthrow a government in order to replace it with another. Since any attempt to overthrow a government in the Arab world could initiate a cycle of costly violence and simply lead in the end to a similar result, taking the time to plant the seeds of a democratic culture is more rewarding for the time being. The best way to achieve this goal is to suspend slogans for overthrowing dictatorships and to focus instead on demanding gradual democratic reforms.

Such education has helped the Muslim Brotherhood advance its goals (Hamid, 1979), enabling it to build an infrastructure to Islamicize society. Future democratic movements in the region should likewise invest in educating the masses about human rights and democracy in order to initiate long-term change.

Internal Reasons for Kefaya's Decline

In addition to the external pressures on Kefaya, internal problems also caused its decline. In the beginning, Kefaya's structure was a source of strength. Activists of all backgrounds could join Kefaya and participate in its activities. Nevertheless, over time, this structure became a liability. One analyst commented,

> The movement made mistakes and began to regress when parties and groups joined it. The founding charter assumes individual membership so that no overlap or clash between membership in the movement and membership in a party would take place. However, what happened was that the members joined as parties . . . . Consequently, a type of hidden struggle began to take place within the movement since each ideological force and every party wanted to hijack it (Ismael, 2006).

The attempt by and inability of each party to implement its own agenda led to the breakup of the coalition. Older, more-established parties also did not want Kefaya to take credit for a success they wished to claim as the fruit of their long struggle. One Egyptian professor even contended that Kefaya's greatest challenge was not the state but antagonism from all the of parties afraid Kefaya would replace them ("The Internal Crisis Within the Egyptian Kefaya Movement," 2006).

One possible reason support for the movement eventually waned was its disconnect with average Egyptians, most of whom live in or near poverty (Kinckmeyer, 2007). Political demands are simply too removed from the basic needs of the average Egyptian (Arafa, 2007). One Kefaya leader who later withdrew from the movement attributed his withdrawal to "the lack of real and effective interaction with the street," as well as Kefaya's attempt to exclude Islamists from the decisionmaking process ("Ma Wara' al-Khabar [Behind the News]," 2006).

A similar complaint was that Kefaya lacked a program that went beyond simply targeting Mubarak. It came across as a movement that "articulates a bitter rejection of the status quo rather than a constructive vision of how it might be transformed" (International Crisis Group, 2005). Some Kefaya sympathizers acknowledge that the demonstrations were "a good idea at the beginning when there were thousands of protesters, but once that number receded, they should have found other means to push for reform" (Al-Shubki, 2007). Kefaya leaders maintained that

> The movement has chosen to focus on its initial goal: "no to extension, no [to] hereditary rule," but that the individual and authoritative nature of presidency in Egypt makes it impossible to bring about any other changes within the structure of the tyrannical ruling regime (Sha'ban, 2006, p. 95).

Moreover, with the "election" of Mubarak and the approval by referendum of the proposed constitutional amendments, the regime and effectively removed Kefaya's stated reasons for existing, which meant it had to begin to look beyond its initial goals.

Observers also argue that Kefaya remained in the "protest phase" for too long. In other words, the organization focused too much on demonstrating and not enough on building a popular base of support. While the more militant wing of Kefaya wished to focus on demonstrations and other direct confrontation of the government, the more moderate (and experienced) wing wished to focus on grassroots, peaceful initiatives. Mohammed Sayyid Said asserts, "Demonstrations are just the first stage. Toppling the regime is not a priority. We need to rebuild democratic institutions in villages and cities . . . trade unions, labor unions, and local assemblies" (author interview, May 2007).

Moreover, in protesting current Egyptian leadership, Kefaya did not offer an alternative strategy that might have helped sustain the organization's credibility. Kefaya also alienated for a time the old political forces of Egypt. For example, Kefaya accused established opposition parties such as Tagammu of being part of the problem with Egyptian politics and not part of the solution (for which it was rebuked by the Tagammu chairman), though it is also possible that competition between the two groups for members led to this internal conflict (author interview, May 2007).

Unlike Islamic groups such as the Muslim Brotherhood, Kefaya also faced financial challenges. The Muslim Brotherhood has claimed that it relies on donations from individual members (Hamid, 1979). Kefaya was also financed by individual donations, but these donations were meager compared to those received by the Islamic parties. Kefaya accepted no foreign funding to maintain its legitimacy and avoid accusations that it was serving foreign interests (Caten, 2005).

Lessons for a Future Kefaya

Some Kefaya leaders have discussed reinventing the movement. If they are to be successful, they will need to learn from their prior experience, including the following four lessons.

First, a revitalized Kefaya will need a well-defined institutional structure, organized hierarchical leadership, and clear membership requirements. It will need to better define its program. Kefaya was alternately praised and condemned by Islamists and secularists alike. The movement was ambiguous in its program.

Kefaya's architects realize that the movement is too ambiguous in its current form. Sha'ban (2006, p. 243) writes that the movement needs to "activate its membership which includes thousands of members who desire to work on creating positive areas of operation"; "reach all areas of Egyptian society—outside the capital city of Cairo"; and "strengthen the pillars of the democratic structure and the ideal that Kefaya has presented about itself." Yet to date, there have been no indications that a new Kefaya would pursue such reforms.

Second, Kefaya should seek alliances with others having practical demands. The only group that has succeeded in obtaining recognition by and response from the Egyptian government has been the workers. Kefaya is credited for having inspired labor protests, with some Egyptian intellectuals believing it "opened or illuminated the way for the workers and revealed that they are the real and non-politicized force able to fill the streets and motivate the authorities to respond to their demands" (Arafa, 2007). The workers are considered to be the spearhead or vehicle aiming for real political and economic reform. Their demands are legitimate—e.g., a basic living wage—and apolitical; hence, they do not automatically alienate the government. Unlike Kefaya, their rhetoric is not political (Al-Shubki, 2007). Kefaya can learn from this experience. By focusing on practical demands that have a broad base of support, Kefaya may be able to activate large numbers of workers and other members and avoid ideological clashes that waste energy and weaken the movement.

Third, Kefaya may need to learn how to work with sympathetic members of the government. From its origin, Kefaya was characterized by a deep-rooted mistrust of the government. Kefaya's secretaries-general publicly expressed this mistrust. The first secretary-general stated repeatedly, "We do not trust the regime or any of the laws that it puts forward" ("George Ishaq: The Ambiguity Is Deliberate to Achieve the Goals of the Regime," n.d.). Kefaya's second secretary-general, Al-Messiri, also continually discredited the government as a whole ("Weak Turnout for the Referendum of the Constitutional Amendments in Egypt," n.d.). Such expressions of mistrust have alienated Kefaya from the ruling party.

While this mistrust is well founded, Kefaya could perhaps better serve its cause by working with the government at times rather than against it at all times. One observer of Egyptian politics writes,

> There are many forces of reform within institutions of the government that are displeased with the corruption and mismanagement. They want to adopt a system that is more proficient, honest and which institutionalizes internal competition between the various branches (Al-Shubki, 2007).

Similarly, the International Crisis Group (2005) recommends Kefaya engage the "reform-minded members of the ruling National Democratic Party."

Fourth, Kefaya would perhaps be more effective if it educated more and protested less. Kefaya leaders believe "the street demonstrations were the most important means to spread its ideas" (Sha'ban, 2006, p. 244). Nevertheless, it needs to develop other means for propagating long-term change. Perhaps it could establish a volunteer education program to teach civil liberties. Even more urgent is the problem of illiteracy, which is near 30 percent for the total adult population and more than 40 percent for women (Central Intelligence Agency, 2008). Some experts suggest that Kefaya should imitate the Islamists who have invested in education and built institutions within a society that would later be receptive to their politics. For the Muslim Brotherhood, education and infrastructure preceded demands for political actions.

CHAPTER FIVE

Conclusions and Implications for U.S. Policy

While the Kefaya movement, like other pro-democracy movements in the region, did not last long or yield many long-lasting results, it nonetheless embodied the strong desire of many in the Middle East for democratic reform. As Rami Khouri (2007), a well-known Jordanian journalist and chief editor of the English-language Lebanese newspaper *Daily Star*, writes,

> The Arab region remains the world's last collectively non-democratic region, having resisted repeated attempts by Arab democrats, liberals, human rights activists, Islamists and constitutionalists to bring their societies into the growing club of democracies around the world . . . Arabs remain eager to participate in the current wave. However, they are not part of today's democratic trend, because Arab political systems remain firmly in the hands of soft hereditary monarchies or brutal security states. Nevertheless, Arab democrats and liberals persist.

The United States, at least in rhetoric, has expressed support for such a move toward democracy. Yet a range of U.S. interests in Egypt and the Middle East, some of which do not encourage direct pressure for Egyptian political reform, has circumscribed U.S. actions. Before considering policies that the United States might adopt to support democratic reform more effectively, we review perceptions of the United States in the Middle East, for these can affect U.S. options at least as much as domestic political conditions within Middle Eastern nations.

Perceptions of the United States

Perceptions can have a strong impact on reality, regardless of whether or not they are based in truth. In the Middle East, popular perception of the United States is generally negative. The prevalent opinion is that the United States is a power that has no or little interest in the welfare of the local populations of other countries, that actively supports dictatorships and hinders democracy, and that has invaded sovereign states unlawfully. U.S. support of Israel is also an ongoing cause for grievance. U.S. demand for Arab oil is perceived to be the primary motivation for the democratic rhetoric and initiatives of the United States in the region (Sha'ban, 2006). Sha'ban (2006, p. 32), reflecting Arab intellectual opinion, writes,

> Democracy is something eagerly awaited at the popular level in our Middle Eastern countries. However, it can be dealt no more damaging blows than when the United States raises its democratic banners and slogans. The U.S. occupies a large Arab country (Iraq) and plunders its wealth. It supports the Zionist uproar in Palestine. How can it propose a program for reform? How could anyone believe the U.S. or its claims? Reality always exposes lies. People know very well that the U.S. has been the main supporter and guardian of the dictatorial regimes which have oppressed us. These regimes have maintained their existence in every instance through U.S. support and because of U.S. interests.

Similarly, al-Sayied (2004, p. 69) claims,

> A sense of lack of stability and security has been spreading recently due to the publicly-declared intimidations and threats from the United States. This feeling is becoming more prevalent due to the interventions by the Bush (Jr.) [sic] administration in internal Arab affairs.

The general public shares a general distrust of the United States. Surveys have consistently found most Arabs identify the United States as the biggest threat to the region and feel that the United States is more interested in controlling oil than spreading democracy (Lobe,

2008). One reason for the perceived insincerity of the United States is its seeming blindness to abuses of human rights by authoritarian regimes that serve its interests, while other regimes that challenge the United States "are singled out for violating democratic precepts, often times subjected to diplomatic and economic sanctions, or in the cases of Afghanistan and Iraq, invaded and occupied" (Baroudi, 2007).

Frustration and anger have grown over the years, and extremism against the United States and Israel has taken many forms. It has also been translated into fear. Sha'ban (2006, p. 58) writes,

> The sense of being victimized by a bigger power is rooted in fact. The elite, consciously or subconsciously, perpetuate this fear. The Arab nation currently faces a set of challenges which constitute a real threat to its physical and cultural existence. These clearly indicate that it is targeted—in a direct, violent, premeditated and systematic fashion. There is nothing ambiguous about it. It is not possible to be confused. They [members of the Arab nation] are targeted on their land. Their riches, holy places, liberty, independence and futures are targeted. The future of coming generations is likewise targeted.

The American invasion of Iraq has also served to further destroy the image of the United States in the region as a democracy broker. In addition to its perceived defiance of international law in invading Iraq, the failure of the U.S. government to create a democracy in Iraq (or even to stabilize the nation) has served only to undermine U.S. ability and integrity. Marina Ottaway (2008) points out that in Iraq, as in elsewhere in the Arab world, the U.S. government has mastered "high flying rhetoric" without any evidence of application on the ground. In fact,

> Holding up Iraq as a model of democratic transformation long after this was plausible, Washington helped convince many in the Arab world that "democracy promotion" was only a euphemism for forcible regime change (Ottaway, 2008).

Even more dangerous, such rhetoric created a backlash against democracy as stories of human-rights abuses by U.S. soldiers, such as those at the Abu Ghraib prison, perpetuated in the Arab media.

In other instances, Arab intellectuals lament that the United States is easily manipulated by regimes that "brilliantly employ the Islamists to scare both local and international communities of the possibility that Islamists could take hold of the country" and thereby waylay demands for reform. Some regional governments have mastered an ability to ignite anti-American and anti-"crusader" sentiment, encouraging demonstrations such as those that occurred over Danish newspaper cartoons that defamed the prophet Muhammad and demonstrated the "danger" that Islam faces from the West (Hasan, 2007).

Negative perceptions of the United States have made it virtually impossible for reformers to turn to it for help. To deal with these perceptions, it is important to understand from where they stem.

It is ironic that U.S. "allies" are perhaps the primary promoters of the image of the United States as a threat to the region. While the Egyptian government, for example, accepts U.S. aid, conducts cooperative military exercises, and supports—at least tacitly—U.S. foreign policy aims in the region, it has vilified the United States to the Egyptian people. For decades, ruling regimes in the Middle East have blamed the lack of reform and democracy on the need to deal with the more urgent issue of "the Zionist-American danger" (Hasan, 2007). Those who are believed to be associated with this enemy are severely punished by these regimes, especially in Egypt. Even though the Mubarak regime is friendly with the United States and the West (and even has a U.S.-brokered peace treaty with Israel), it has not hesitated to prosecute intellectuals who call for reform, charging they are furthering the U.S. or the Israeli agenda. Kefaya activists have been among those labeled as "American agents" by the government (Human Rights Watch, 2005b). As a result, even liberal secularists who would like to see the emergence of a U.S.-style political system in the Arab world are careful to disassociate themselves from the United States. Many reformers find themselves regurgitating a rhetorical attack on the United States in order to sound patriotic and avoid being prosecuted for spreading liberal "American" ideas such as democracy.

The regimes that control most of the media in the Arab world have given a platform to those who perpetuate anti-American positions. Human rights violations committed by the U.S. armed forces at the Abu Ghraib and Guantanamo prisons are still mentioned almost daily in the Arab media, providing fodder for those who decry U.S. intentions in the region. Arabs who lived under European colonial rule for decades fear another Western colonization, this time by the United States. Arab regimes perpetuate this notion, as when former Lebanese Prime Minister Salim al-Hoss stated that U.S. intervention in the region is comparable to the foreign intervention that dominated the region under different names such as "colonization," "mandate," and "protectorate" (Abushi, 2007). The forces of colonization are believed to be "taking turns in this occupation and destruction—between the European-American century which has passed and the Zionist-American century which has begun" in which the United States is feared to be "ripping apart" whatever the European colonization did not destroy (Ahmed et al., 2006, p. 178).

By demonizing the United States, many Middle Eastern regimes have successfully deflected attention from their own failed governance. Local populations seem to be more preoccupied with external politics, such as destructive U.S. policies in the region, than local issues, such as improving protection of human rights. Our analysis of the Arabic-language media found a firmly held belief in the Arab world that unless the U.S. threat is dealt with, no reform or democracy can take hold.

The complex relationship between Egypt and the United States highlights the full range of issues that must be addressed by U.S. efforts to boost democracy in the Middle East. While the Executive Branch of the U.S. government professes an interest in Egyptian political reform, it also aggressively protects its relationship with Egypt from any serious interference by Congress and lauds Egyptian cooperation even when that involves the abuse of human rights and the curtailing of democratic freedoms. At the same time, the Egyptian government, which enjoys U.S. military and economic aid, maligns U.S. foreign policies and brands reformers with charges of collaborating in a U.S. infiltration of the country. U.S. unwillingness to fully press for reforms thus suggests to the Egyptian people that the United States engages Egypt only to secure the hegemony of Israel and Egyptian cooperation with the U.S. military. By failing to fully press for reform, the United States has failed to buttress Egyptian reformers in the face of attacks by the Mubarak regime, while also providing the regime with further fodder for its anti-American sloganeering and branding. Meanwhile, Egypt's refusal to make political reform a priority means that the United States must continually press for reform without really meaning it, mainly in order to satisfy domestic concerns but also in the belief that strong, successful societies are less likely to produce or be destabilized by violent extremism.

Policy Recommendations

Given the constraints placed by public opinion in the Middle East on U.S. policy, what can the United States do to promote democratic reform? What can Arab democrats do to help themselves?

First, the United States stands to gain in the long run if it pursues a consistent policy of support for democratic reform efforts and reformers in the Arab world. The U.S. government already supports reform efforts through organizations such as the U.S. Agency for International Development and the United Nations Development Programme. Given the current negative popular standing of the Untied States in the region, U.S. support for reform initiatives is best carried out through nongovernmental and nonprofit institutions.

International pressure on authoritarian regimes sometimes works. Through its media outlets, the United States could help create a platform for reformers by publicly endorsing their efforts. Such policies would send a clear signal over time to both the regimes and the populations that while the United States values its partnership with the regimes, it also values those who advocate democracy. Such actions could help protect such movements and individuals from repression and intimidation.

Second, the United States should develop the means to better assess and understand local political conditions and to assess the reform movements that arise within this environment. Due to the deep misunderstanding of the concept of secularism, purely secular political movements currently appeal to only a narrow segment of Egyptian and other Arab societies. Islamist opposition movements present a particular challenge to the United States, as these are sometimes among the most significant and locally credible voices for change. There are many shades of opinion within and among Islamist parties and a wide spectrum of views on reform and democracy among them. The United States can gain valuable insights by communicating with all movements and parties that eschew violence and seek peaceful change. Engaging such groups does not, of course, necessarily mean supporting them. To the extent that the United States is seen to be open to dialogue with all shades of peaceful reformist opinion, its support for democratization in the region will be viewed as less narrowly self-serving and more genuine.

Reform movements also need external support to withstand the pressures on them. Kefaya was inspired by similar movements, such as the Orange Revolution, and it also inspired others to follow in its footsteps. But the local nature of the Kefaya movement made it difficult for it to survive internal pressure. Developing external sources of support for Kefaya or other pro-democracy groups may help them weather periods of repression. Creating links to other pro-democracy groups may also provide these organizations with additional resources, both financial and intellectual. For example, many would argue the Muslim Brotherhood's network outside of Egypt has helped it flourish despite some state persecution.

Creating external support networks can also be beneficial to other reform-oriented groups, such as journalists. Therefore, the U.S. government should consider supporting organizations that help sustain journalists and bloggers. There is no question that the media played a role in Kefaya's success and also in its decline. The media can have an integral part to play in pressuring governments to tolerate reform efforts.

More broadly, the U.S. government should help foster international pressure against the persecution of reformers. Western and international policymakers should intervene on behalf of detained leaders of reform groups. Helping these individuals obtain a higher international profile will make it more difficult to marginalize them.

By facilitating transnational connections, the U.S. government and nongovernmental organizations can also encourage reform movements to develop their own international or transnational messages. Kefaya imitators in other Arab nations, for example, could help the movement become a transnational one. This would allow it to continue despite local censorship by maintaining planning and leadership beyond the reach of any one government and its security agencies. This is similar to the strategy many Islamic extremists use, and it would help reformers be more effective in opposing them.

Third, the U.S. government should encourage nongovernmental organizations to offer training to reformers, including guidance on coalition building and how to deal with internal differences in pursuit of democratic reform. Academic institutions (or even nongovernmental organizations associated with U.S. political parties, such as the International Republican Institute or the National Democratic Institute for International Affairs) could carry out such training, which would equip reform leaders to reconcile their differences peacefully and democratically.

Fourth, the United States should help reformers obtain and use information technology, perhaps by offering incentives for U.S. companies to invest in the region's communications infrastructure and information technology. U.S. information technology companies could also help ensure that the Web sites of reformers can remain in operation and could invest in technologies such as anonymizers that could offer some shelter from government scrutiny. This could also be accomplished by employing technological safegaurds to prevent regimes from sabotaging the Web sites of reformers.

Kefaya was initially successful in part because of its ability to exploit communication technology. The ability of activists to document and expose human-rights abuses forced the government to prosecute some of the perpetrators of these acts (Maqlad, 2007). "This tool," al-Maliky (2007) contended, "has already resulted in a loss of control for autocracy since bloggers have exposed human-rights abuses by the state." Many of these blogs became well known and enjoyed a surprising record of success. This did not go unnoticed by the state, which began to persecute some bloggers.

Disseminating the messages of reformers in international forums, especially cultural ones, can help thwart state repression. It is important to build dissident leaders into more widely recognized personalities who can counterbalance the perceived "heroism" of jihadists. Such reformers need a platform, including translation and dissemination of their works. They should be linked with civil-society supporters elsewhere to provide international exposure to their message. They also need to be educated on the international ideological context of their work so that they can craft messages that will be accurately understood.

Fifth, as noted previously for Kefaya, the United States should help reformers foster effective social-service programs to enable them to build a constituency and make inroads into urban and rural environments that have been claimed by extremists. Offering education, health care, and financial support can help build strong relationships on local levels, relationships that may be later leveraged into political support and recruitment. The United States should also seek ways to help these groups with long-term strategic thinking about their role in pressing for democratic reform. Kefaya perhaps spent too much time protesting and too little time mobilizing. The call for effective social services is as much about providing health care as it as about social investment—social services must be packaged with a strategy for reform and engagement. Reformers belong to the same social and educational stratum that, in other places, has been instrumental in the building of civil society. They should be encouraged and provided with the resources to make themselves materially useful to the public.

Meeting the needs of individuals and communities at the grassroots level has proven to be an effective method for gaining the public's trust and influence. The adversaries of democracy are adept at exploiting that trust to exert ideological influence that pulls people toward radical parties and movements, as ongoing RAND research on the provision of social services demonstrates. But successful antisectarian and antiviolence movements have also begun by providing social services at the grassroots level and developed from there into a more political effort, as ongoing RAND research on women's civic organizations in areas of conflict also demonstrates. The excessively intellectual, theoretical nature of some Middle Eastern democracy movements could be counterbalanced by stronger links to the real, everyday needs of the population. While it is true that they are likely to be out-spent by the extremists and fundamentalists, who have strong funding streams at their disposal, the successful role of civil-society groups in helping to resolve conflicts in Ireland, the Balkans, and Argentina demonstrates that this is not a deal breaker. What matters is the connection to neighborhoods and communities that results from grassroots service provision, even if it is very modest.

Conclusion

The United States should improve its capacity for positive engagement in the Arab world. Fortunately, it is possible for the United States to play a very constructive role in the region. Most Arabs are eager for change. As Jamil Matar (2007) writes, "We Arabs want our hearts to rest assured that the period of time is limited and not open-ended—that democracy is waiting for us at the end of the tunnel."

The prospects for democratization seem promising in Egypt, where a sizable majority of the population seeks reform. The very creation of Kefaya "signals a crucial change in Egypt's political mood, in stark contrast with the stagnation that has dominated for years" (El-Anani, 2005). It is critical that movements like Kefaya be read as healthy political expressions rather than as a "bunch of agitators bent on trouble-making" and as demonstrating "that the Egyptian society remains capable of producing new leaders" (El-Anani, 2005). Kefaya's choice of peaceful methods was quite significant, as was its rapid mobilization of students, lawyers, and writers, indicating how widespread the desire for change actually is. Many intellectuals believe that if reforms are not implemented and the desire for democracy addressed in the very near future, "absolute chaos" will take hold of the country because those who see no hope of reforming the system will aim to destroy it altogether (Al-Shubki, 2007). While most regimes in the region remain quite strong and such comments may represent more hyperbole than truth, encouraging reform through peaceful means will lessen the credibility of violent options.

Since the introduction of President Bush's Freedom Agenda in his 2003 speech to the National Endowment for Democracy, there has been mounting criticism from within the United States and internationally regarding the U.S. pursuance of democracy in the Middle East. It is noteworthy that the anti-Americanism of some Kefaya members and other opposition groups stems from U.S. actions elsewhere in the Middle East. The United States may have to recognize that a truly democratic movement will likely reflect the sentiments of the people it seeks to represent, in which case, an Egyptian movement would likely deploy anti-American rhetoric, as indeed does the Egyptian government when that suits its purposes. The stance of Kefaya or some other pro-democracy group may be at odds with some U.S. positions, such as those on Iraq and Palestine; even so, this type of reform movement, if effective, can prove beneficial in the end if the reforms it engenders ultimately promote a more intellectually and economically vigorous (and militarily stable) region.

Violence has been used in an attempt to bring about political change in the Middle East for some time. Arabs are keenly aware that only when "this violence was transported to the U.S. was it transformed into a critical challenge that needs to be addressed" (BilQzeez, 2007, p. 51). Many are alarmed that the United States appears to be addressing democratic reform as a security issue. BilQzeez (2007, p. 51) writes

> The U.S. is using the same approach the Arab regimes used to solve this problem after it had already failed to address this phenomenon. This approach focuses on the issue of security without addressing the deep motivations behind these practices. The measures taken by Arabs against these activities were brutal but failed to produce real results. Ironically, the more aggressive the Arabic regimes have been in dealing with violent groups, the more violence they have attracted. This violence has come in increasingly aggressive waves and a cycle of escalating brutality was created.

It is therefore critical that the United States couch its support for democracy in the Middle East in terms likely to appeal to the local populations and work with its allies to build the infrastructure needed to initiate democracy in its fullest form. As Tarabishi (1998, p. 27) points out, "democracy is not a ripe fruit ready for the picking." Rather, it is a seed ready to be planted that must be carefully cultivated in order to bear fruit. Sometimes, this may occur many years later.

References

"83% Voted in Favor of Amending the Constitution; The Journalists Union and Kefaya Accuse the National Party of Egypt of Sexual Molestation [83 bi al-mi'a sawwatu li salih tacdil al-dustur. niqabat al-suhufiyyin wa Kefaya tattahiman al-hizb al-watani fi misr bi al-taharrush al-jinsi']," Alarabiya.net, May 25, 2005.[1] As of May 3, 2007:
http://www.alarabiya.net/articles/2005/05/25/13361.html

Abbas, Wael, "A Special Report on the Imprisonment of Aiman Nour," Misrdigital.blogspirit.com, December 31, 2005. As of February 1, 2008:
http://misrdigital.blogspirit.com/archive/2005/12/index.html

———, "Egyptian Consciousness [al-waci al-masri]," September 24, 2007. As of September 26, 2007:
http://misrdigital.blogspirit.com

Abd Al-Llah, Mohammed, "The Kefaya Movement Organizes a Protest with Brooms in Front of al-Sayyida Zaynab [harakat Kefaya tunaththim ihtijajan bi al-makanis 'amama al-sayyida zaynab]," Masrawy.com, June 15, 2005. As of April 13, 2007:
http://masrawy.com/News/2005/MidEast/Reuters/June/15/OEGTP-EGYPT-KEFAYAH-MM57782240.aspx

Abdalla, Ahmed, "Egypt's Islamists and the State: From Complicity to Confrontation," *Middle East Report*, No. 183, July/August 1993, pp. 28–31.

Abdel-Latif, Omayma, "Dreaming of Better Times," *Al-Ahram Weekly*, November 23–29, 2000. As of January 31, 2008:
http://weekly.ahram.org.eg/2000/509/eg2.htm

Abushi, Ayman, "At the Seventh Doha Forum on Democracy, Development and Free Trade [fi muntada al-dawha al-sabic li al-dimuqratiyya wa al-tanmiya wa al-tijara al-hurra]," Raya.com, April 2007. As of May 24, 2007:

[1] Translations and transliterations of title in this list of references were performed by the author.

http://www.raya.com/site/topics/article.
asp?cu_no=2&item_no=244533&version=1&template_id=20&parent_id=19.

Ahmed, Youssef, et al., *Requirements for Reform in the Arab World* ["mutatallibat al-'islah fi al-calam al-carabi]," Amman: Arab Institution and Abd al-Hamid Shuman Institution, 2006.

Al-Anani, Khalil, "The Kefaya Movement Depicted as a Social Phenomenon [harakat Kefaya bi wasfiha thahira mujtamaciyya]," *al-Quds al-Arabi*, May 15, 2005a. As of February 1, 2008:
http://www.elkarama.net/modules.php?name=News&file=article&sid=342

———, "Egypt: Parliamentary Elections in the Shadow of 2000," *Arab Reform Bulletin*, Vol. 3, No. 8, October 2005b, Washington, D.C.: Carnegie Endowment for International Peace, p. 3.

Al-Aryan, Isam, "The Constitutional Amendments in Egypt and Extent of Presence of the 'Brotherhood' in Democratic Institutions" [*al-tacdilat al-dusturiyya fi misr wa mada hudur "al-'ikhwan" fi al-mu'assasat al-dimuqratiyya*], Daralhayat.com, April 8, 2007. As of February 1, 2008:
http://www.daralhayat.com/special/issues/04-2007/Item-20070407-cd09a1b8-c0a8-10ed-01d5-2634d737529b/story.html

Al-Kuwari, Ali, ed., *The Crisis of Democracy in Arab Countries: Objections to and Reservations About Democracy in the Arab World* [*'azmat al-dimuqratiyya fi al-buldan al-carabiyya—'ictiradat wa tahaffuthat cala al-dimuqratiyya fi al-calam al-carabi*], London: Dar Al Saqi, 2004.

Al-Malky, Rania, "Blogging for Reform: The Case for Egypt," Arabmediasociety.spgd.co.uk, February 1, 2007. As of September 25, 2007:
http://arabmediasociety.sqgd.co.uk/topics/index.php?t_article=39

Al-Misri, Mohammed, "Kefaya Demonstration Calls for Not Voting for Mubarak. Civilian Report Describes the Media as Biased Toward the Candidate of the Ruling Party [tathahura li harakat Kefaya tadcu li cadam al-taswit li mubarak. taqrir madani yasif wasa'il al-'iclam bi al-inhiyaz li murashshah al-hizb al-hakim]," Alarabiya.net, September 9, 2005. As of May 3, 2007:
http://www.alarabiya.net/articles/2005/09/07/16566.html

Al-Sa'dawi, Nawal, "Craftiness in the Thought of the Egyptian Elite [al-murawagha fi fikr al-nukhab al-misriyya]," Al-araby.com, February 2007. As of October 29, 2007:
http://www.al-araby.com/articles/1044/070204-1044-opn07.htm

Al-Sayied, Radhwan, *An Essay on the Arab Political Reform* ["maqala fi al-'islah al-siyasi al-carabi]," Beirut, Lebanon: Dar al-Nahar Publishing House, 2004.

Al-Shubki, Amer, "And They Are the Revolution of the People [wa hum al-thawra al-shacbiyya]," Al-masry-alyoum.com, May 10, 2007. As of January 31, 2008:
http://208.109.248.104/article.aspx?ArticleID=56946

Al-Sultan, Mahmoud, "The Egyptian 'Kefaya' Movement—The Rose Growing in Salty Soil! [harakat Kefaya al-misriyya—'idh tanbut al-warda fi 'ard malih]," *Majalat al-Asr*, April 3, 2005. As of January 31, 2008: http://www.alasr.ws/index.cfm?method=home.con&contentID=6517

Arafa, Mohammed Gamal, "The Workers: 'Spearhead' of the Political Movement in Egypt [al-cummal "ra's harbat" al-hirak al-siyasi fi misr]," Islamonline.net, May 9, 2007. As of October 29, 2007: http://www.islamonline.net/servlet/Satellite?c=ArticleA_C&cid=1178723961215&pagename=Zone-Arabic-News/NWALayout

Baroudi, Sami, "Arab Intellectuals and the Bush Administration's Campaign for Democracy: The Case of the Greater Middle East Initiative," *The Middle East Journal*, Vol. 61, No. 3, Summer 2007.

Basheer, Tahseen, "The Egyptian State in Transition," in Phebe Marr, ed., *Egypt at the Crossroads: Domestic Stability and Regional Role*, Washington, D.C.: National Defense University Press, 1999, pp. 3–16. As of January 30, 2008: http://www.ndu.edu/inss/books/books%20-%201999/Egypt%20at%20the%20Crossroads%20-%20June%2099/ECDS.pdf

"Benefits from the Experience of the Kefaya Movement of Egypt. Libyans Launch the 'Khalas' Movement as an Expression of their Rejection of al-Qaddafi [istifadat bi tajribat harakat Kefaya fi misr. libiyyun yutliqun harakat "khalas" tacbiran can rafdihim li al-qadhdhafi]," Alarabiya.net, April 3, 2005. As of February 1, 2008: http://www.alarabiya.net/articles/2005/04/03/11852.html

BilQzeez, Abd Alilah, *On Political Reform and Democracy* [*fi al-'islah al-siyasi wa al-dimuqratiyya*], Beirut, Lebanon: Al-Sharika al-cAlamiya Li al-Kitab Publishing House, 2007.

Brinkley, Joel, and Richard W. Stevenson, "Bush Welcomes Gaza Plan, Without Backing It Fully," *New York Times*, April 13, 2004. As of January 30, 2008: http://query.nytimes.com/gst/fullpage.html?res=9B00E3DD1F38F930A25757C0A9629C8B63

Brown, Nathaniel, and Michele Dunne, "Egypt's Controversial Constitutional Amendments: A Textual Analysis," Carnegie Endowment for Peace, March 23, 2007.

Bureau of Economic Analysis, "U.S. International Trade in Goods and Services," June 8, 2007.

"Campaign to Free the Brave Egyptian Blogger AbdelKareem nabil Soliman," Freekareem.org, September 16, 2007. As of September 27, 2007: http://www.freekareem.org

Cardenas, Sonia, and Andrew Flibbert, "National Human Rights Institutions in the Middle East," *The Middle East Journal*, Vol. 59, No. 3, Summer 2005.

Caten, George, "The Egyptian Movement—Kefaya—Going Beyond Ideological Parties [harakat Kefaya al-misriyya tatajawaz al-'ahzab al-'aydiyulujiyya]," *Civilized Dialogue*, No. 1238, June 24, 2005. As of January 31, 2008:
http://www.ahewar.org/debat/show.art.asp?aid=39870

Central Intelligence Agency, *The World Factbook*, 2008. As of February 1, 2008:
https://www.cia.gov/library/publications/the-world-factbook/index.html

"Clinton Discusses Military Strikes," transcription of Presidential address, Online News Hour, August 20, 1998. As of January 30, 2008:
http://www.pbs.org/newshour/bb/military/july-dec98/clinton2_8-20.html

"The Corruption File," August 26, 2006. As of May 27, 2008:
http://harakamasria.org/?q=node/7368

"Detainment of Kefaya Leaders and Members ['ictiqal qiyadat wa 'acda' min harakat Kefaya]," Ournormandy.com, July 30, 2005. As of February 1, 2008:
http://www.ournormandy.com/forum/showthread.php?t=2079

Dunne, Michele Durocher, "Evaluating Egyptian Reform," Carnegie Endowment for International Peace, Carnegie Papers No. 66, January 2006. As of January 31, 2008:
http://www.carnegieendowment.org/files/CP66.Dunne.FINAL.pdf

"Egypt: Strike over IMF Privatization Policies," PeaceNet, 1994. As of January 30, 2008:
http://www.africa.upenn.edu/Govern_Political/egt_imf.html

Egyptian Movement for Change, "Establishment of National Front for Change," October 10, 2005. As of January 31, 2008:
http://harakamasria.org/node/3148

"The Egyptian Organization Demands the Immediate Release of Protestors of the Kefaya Movement [al-munaththama al-misriyya tutalib bi al-'ifraj al-fawri can mutathahiri harakat kefaya]," Hrinfo.net, July 31, 2005. As of May 24, 2007:
http://hrinfo.net/egypt/eohr/2005/pr0731.shtml

"Egyptians Against Torture [misriyyun didda al-tacdhib]," Harakamasria.org, September 9, 2007. As of September 27, 2007:
http://harakamasria.org/?q=node/9736

El-Anani, Khalil, "Resurrecting the Body Politic," *Al-Ahram Weekly*, September 8–14, 2005, No. 759. As of February 1, 2008:
http://weekly.ahram.org.eg/2005/759/op9.htm

El-Din, Gamal Essam, "Space to Say 'No' to the President," *Al-Ahram Weekly*, December 16–22, 2004. As of January 31, 2008:
http://weekly.ahram.org.eg/2004/721/eg4.htm

El Masri, Ahmad, "Bahb Masr," July 2, 2007. As of September 27, 2007:
http://bahbmasr.blogspot.com/

El-Sayed, Mohammad, "Divided They Stand," *Al-Ahram Weekly*, December 21–27, 2006, No. 825. As of May 4, 2007:
http://weekly.ahram.org.eg/2006/825/eg6.htm

El-Zohery, Mahmoud, "The Kefaya Movement Between National and Religious Forces: Is There Any Relief? [harakat Kefaya bayna al-quwa al-wataniyya wa al-diniyya: hal min infiraja?]," Ssrcaw.org, October 3, 2006. As of June 13, 2007:
http://www.ssrcaw.org/ar/show.art.asp?t=2&aid=77164

"The Events of Several Months of Assaults on Members of the Media [waqa'ic bacd 'ashhur al-'ictida'at cala al-'iclamiyyin]," Asharaqalawsat.com, June 26, 2005. As of April 18, 2007:
http://www.asharqalawsat.com/details.asp?section=1&issue=9707&article=307908

"George Ishaq: The Ambiguity Is Deliberate to Achieve the Goals of the Regime [jurj 'ishaq: al-ghumud maqsud li tamrir 'ahdaf al-nidham]," Alwafdparty.org, n.d. As of March 2007:
http://www.alwafdparty.org/details.aspx?id=449

Gerges, Fawas, "Arab Reservations on Democracy," in Ali Al-Kori, ed., *The Crisis of Democracy in Arab Countries* ["'azmat al-dimuqratiyya fi al-buldan al-carabiyya]," London: Dar al-Saqi Publishing House, 2004.

———, *The Far Enemy: Why Jihad Went Global*, Cambridge, England: Cambridge University Press, 2005.

Hairman180 (posted by), "Police Brutality in Egypt," Youtube.com, posted circa 2006. As of February 1, 2008:
http://www.youtube.com/watch?v=iCHM6LYiBsY.

Hamid, Wala', *What Do You Know About the Muslim Brotherhood? [madha tacrif can al-'ikhwan al-muslimin?]*, Cairo: Kitab al-Mukhtar, 1979.

Hasan, Bahy al-Deen, "Is It Possible to Avoid an Arab 9/11? The Internal Causes for Stagnation of Democracy Building," Cihrs.org, October 1, 2007. As of October 13, 2007:
http://www.cihrs.org/opinion_details_ar.aspx?op_id=159

Hassan, Abd al-Basir, "Kefaya Calls for Forming a Front for Entering the Legislative Elections [Kefaya tadcu li tashkil jibha li khawd al-'intikhabat al-tashriciyya]," BBCArabic.com, September 23, 2005. As of February 1, 2008:
http://news.bbc.co.uk/hi/arabic/middle_east_news/newsid_4273000/4273776.stm

Hedges, Chris, "U.S.-Egypt Ties Are Strained in Detention of Islamic Cleric," *New York Times*, July 7, 1993. As of January 30, 2008:
http://query.nytimes.com/gst/fullpage.html?res=9F0CE6DD143BF934A35754C0A965958260

Howeidy, Amira, "A Chronology of Dissent," *Al-Ahram Weekly*, June 23–29, 2005a. As of February 1, 2008:
http://weekly.ahram.org.eg/2005/748/eg10.htm

———, "Enough Is Still Enough," *Al-Ahram Weekly*, September 8–15, 2005b. As of January 31, 2008:
http://weekly.ahram.org.eg/2005/759/eg8.htm

Human Rights Watch, "Egypt," 1993. As of January 31, 2008:
http://www.hrw.org/reports/1994/WR94/Middle-02.htm#P137_70431

———, "Black Hole: The Fate of Islamists Rendered to Egypt," Vol. 17, No. 5, May 2005a. As of January 30, 2008:
http://www.hrw.org/reports/2005/egypt0505/egypt0505.pdf

———, "Egypt: The Call for Reform is Met with Brutality [misr: al-dacwa li al-'islahat juwajah bi al-wahshiyya]," Hrw.org, May 26, 2005b. As of May 24, 2007:
http://hrw.org/arabic/docs/2005/05/26/egypt11055_txt.htm

Ibrahim, Saad Eddin, "Note from Prison," in *Egypt, Islam and Democracy: Critical Essays*, Cairo: American University of Cairo Press, 2002.

"In the Same Mode as the Egypt Movement and Aiming to Bring About Political Change—Founding of a Sudanese Movement Raising the Banner of 'Kefaya' Without Objection by the Authorities [cala ghirar al-haraka al-misriyya wa tahduf li 'ihdath tahawwul siyasi—ta'sis haraka sudaniyya tarfac shicar 'Kefaya' dun ictirad al-sulutat]," Alarabiya.net, June 3, 2006. As of May 3, 2007:
http://www.alarabiya.net/articles/2006/06/03/24309.html

"The Internal Crisis Within the Egyptian Kefaya Movement [al-'azma al-dakhiliyya fi harakat Kefaya al-misriyya]," al-Jazeera.net, December 16, 2006. As of January 31, 2008:
http://www.aljazeera.net/NR/exeres/ED3EEF37-1CF2-45B5-BF47-D13FE10CDA9F.htm

International Crisis Group, "Reforming Egypt: In Search of a Strategy," October 4, 2005. As of March, 20, 2007:
http://www.crisisgroup.org/library/documents/middle_east___north_africa/egypt_north_africa/46_reforming_egypt_in_search_of_a_strategy.pdf

International Labour Organization, "Egypt," 2006. As of February 1, 2008:
http://www.ilo.org/public/english/region/afpro/cairo/countries/egypt.htm

"Is the Kefaya Movement Changing into a Party? [hal tatahawwal harakat Kefaya 'ila hizb]," Egypty.com, 2004. As of February 1, 2008:
http://www.egypty.com/top4/kefaia_opposition.asp

Ismael, Farraj, "Affirming that He Sympathizes with the Brotherhood and Is Not a Brother [yu'akkid 'annahu mutacatif maca al-'ikhwan wa laysa 'ikhwaniyyan]," Alarabiya.net, November 23, 2005. As of May 3, 2007:
http://www.alarabiya.net/articles/2005/11/23/18883.html

———, "Its General Coordinator Declines Comment for Two Days: The 'Veil' of Farouq Husni Wreaks Havoc on 'Kefaya' and Two Major Figureheads Announce

Its End [munassiqha al-camm yamtanic can al-kalaam yawmayn: 'hijab' faruq husni yacsif bi 'Kefaya' wa ramzan kabiran yuclinun nihayataha]," Alarabiya.net, December 10, 2006. As of May 3, 2007:
http://www.alarabiya.net/articles/2006/12/10/29805.html.

Kassem, Maye, *Egyptian Politics: The Dynamics of Authoritarian Rule*, Boulder, Colo.: Lynne Reiner Publishers, Inc., 2004.

"Kefaya Accuses the Police of Ravishing the Honor of One of Its Activists; a Demonstration in South Korea Demands that the Egyptian President Step Down [kefaya tattahim al-shurta bi intihak card 'ahad nashitiha; muthahara fi kuriya al-janubiyya tutalib bi tanahhi al-ra'is al-misri]," Alarabiya.net, May 26, 2006. As of May 3, 2007:
http://www.alarabiya.net/articles/2006/05/26/24093.html

"The Kefaya Movement—Challenges and Factions [harakat Kefaya—tahaddiyat wa inshiqaqat]," al-Jazeera.net, December 13, 2006. As of May 24, 2007:
http://www.aljazeera.net/Channel/archive/archive?ArchiveId=1035418

"The Kefaya Movement Condemns Terrorism [harakat Kefaya tudin al-'irhab]," Misrdigital.blogspirit.com, April 7, 2005. As of February 1, 2008:
http://misrdigital.blogspirit.com/archive/2005/04/07/

Khalil, Majdi, "Between the Kefaya and Free Officers Movements [bayna harakat Kefaya wa harakat al-dubbat al-'ahrar]," Elaph.com, December 13, 2005. As of February 1, 2008:
http://www.elaph.com/ElaphWeb/ElaphWriter/2005/12/112610.htm

Khouri, Rami G., "The Heroism of Arab Democrats," Middle-east-online.com, May 31, 2007. As of February 2, 2008:
http://www.middle-east-online.com/ENGLISH/?id=20911

Kinckmeyer, Ellen, "In Egypt, a Son Is Readied for Succession: On Streets, Dynasty Viewed as a 'Given,'" *Washington Post*, October 11, 2007. As of October 11, 2007:
http://www.washingtonpost.com/wp-dyn/content/article/2007/10/10/AR2007101002436.html.

"The Labor Party and Youth for Change Withdraw from Kefaya [insihab hizb al-camal wa shabab min 'ajl al-taghyir wa 'akharin min Kefaya]," Demokratia-shaabia.com, December 10, 2006. As of May 24, 2007:
http://www.demokratia-shaabia.com/site/content/show_news.php?subaction=showfull&id=1165957519

Laqueur, Walter, *The Struggle for the Middle East: The Soviet Union in the Mediterranean, 1958–1968*, New York: Macmillan, 1969.

Lobe, Jim, "Poll: Israel, U.S. Greatest Threats to Middle East," April 15, 2008. As of May 27, 2008:
http://electronicintifada.net/v2/article9458.shtml

"Ma Wara' al-Khabar ["Behind the News]," al-Jazeera.net, December 12, 2006. As of October 11, 2008:
http://www.aljazeera.net/NR/exeres/ED3EEF37-1CF2-45B5-BF47-D13FE10CDA9F.htm

Maqlad, Diana, "So We Do Not Lose Electronic Freedom [hatta la nakhsar al-hurriya al-'ilaktuniyya]," Alsharqalawsat.com, June 10, 2007. As of October 31, 2007:
http://www.asharqalawsat.com/leader.asp?section=3&issue=10421&article=422880&search=%D8%A7%D9%84%D8%B6%D8%A7%D8%A8%D8%B7%20%D8%A7%D9%84%D9%85%D8%B5%D8%B1%D9%8A&state=true

Mark, Clyde R., "Egypt–United States Relations," Congressional Research Service Issue Brief, April 2, 2004.

Marr, Phebe, "Egypt at the Crossroads," in Phebe Marr, ed., *Egypt at the Crossroads: Domestic Stability and Regional Role*, Washington, D.C.: National Defense University Press, 1999, pp. 231–252. As of January 30, 2008:
http://www.ndu.edu/inss/books/books%20-%201999/Egypt%20at%20the%20Crossroads%20-%20June%2099/ECDS.pdf

Matar, Jamil, "Enjoyable Conversations About Democracy in Petra [hiwarat mumtica fi al-batra' can al-dimuqratiyya]," Alhayat.com, June 4, 2007. As of June 12, 2007:
http://www.daralhayat.com/opinion/06-2007/Item-20070603-f26c84e1-c0a8-10ed-01b1-6996527fbbbb/story.html

McConnell, Kathryn, "Bush Signs $20.9 Billion Foreign Aid Spending Measure," U.S. Department of State, November 15, 2005. As of January 30, 2008:
http://www.america.gov/st/washfile-english/2005/November/20051114154933AKllennoCcM0.9979517.html

Mohamed from Cairo, "Kefaya's Momentum for Change," Fromcairo.blogspot.com, May 21, 2005. As of September 27, 2007:
http://fromcairo.blogspot.com/2005/05/kefayas-momentum-for-change.html

"Mubarak Warns of '100 bin Ladens,'" Reuters, March 31, 2003. As of January 30, 2008:
http://www.cnn.com/2003/WORLD/meast/03/31/iraq.egypt.mubarak.reut/

Office of the United Nations High Commissioner for Human Rights, "Human Rights Experts Concerned over Attacks on Egyptian Judiciary," June 14, 2006. As of September 28, 2007:
http://www.unhchr.ch/huricane/huricane.nsf/0/30D0AEC974F20B6EC125718D005FF0F7?opendocument

Organisation for Economic Co-operation and Development, *African Economic Outlook, 2005–2006*, Paris, May 2006.

Ottaway, Marina, "Democracy Promotion in the Middle East: Restoring Credibility," 2008. As of June 9, 2008:
http://www.carnegieendowment.org/files/pb_60_ottaway_final.pdf

Owen, Roger, "A New Post–Cold War System? The Middle East in a Realigned World," *Middle East Report*, No. 184, September/October 1993, pp. 2–6.

Pannell, Ian, "Egypt Angry at US Rights Comments," News.bbc.co.uk, September 26, 2007. As of February 1, 2008:
http://news.bbc.co.uk/2/hi/middle_east/7014994.stm

Quandt, William B., *The United States and Egypt: An Essay on Policy for the 1990s*, Washington, D.C.: Brookings Institution, 1990.

"The Role of Scholars and the Issue of Legacy of the Prophets ['adwar al-culama' wa mas'alat al-wiratha al-nabawiyya]," Daralhayat.com, June 9, 2007. As of October 29, 2007:
http://www.daralhayat.com/classics/06-2007/Item-20070608-0c2f7e0d-c0a8-10ed-01b1-6996f3dc2b2b/story.html

Said Aly, Abdel Moneim, "Egypt-U.S. Relations and Egyptian Foreign Policy," Washington Institute for Near East Policy, PolicyWatch #448, March 24, 2000. As of January 30, 2008:
http://www.washingtoninstitute.org/templateC05.php?CID=1326

Said Aly, Abdel Moneim, and Robert H. Pelletreau, "U.S.-Egyptian Relations," *Middle East Policy*, Vol. 8, No. 2, June 2001, pp. 45–58.

Satloff, Robert, "U.S. Policy Toward Egypt," testimony before the U.S. House Committee on International Affairs, April 10, 1997. As of January 30, 2008:
http://www.washingtoninstitute.org/templateC07.php?CID=27

Sayigh, Yezid, and Avil Shalim, eds., *The Cold War and the Middle East*, Oxford, England: Clarendon Press, 1997.

Schemm, Paul, "Egypt Struggles to Control Anti-War Protests," *Middle East Report Online*, March 31, 2003. As of September 6, 2007:
http://www.merip.org/mero/mero033103.html

Sha'ban, Ahmed Baha' al-Din, *The Butterfly Effect: Kefaya—Past and Present*, Cairo: Kefaya Printings, 2006.

Shadid, Anthony, "Egypt Shuts Door on Dissent as U.S. Officials Back Away," *Washington Post*, March 19, 2007. As of February 1, 2008:
http://www.washingtonpost.com/wp-dyn/content/article/2007/03/18/AR2007031801196.html

Sharib, Haydar, "Egyptian Youth Demand Change [al-shabab al-misri yutalib al-taghyir]," BBCArabic.com, August 2, 2005. As of February 1, 2008:
http://news.bbc.co.uk/hi/arabic/middle_east_news/newsid_4738000/4738685.stm

Shorbagy, Manar, "Understanding Kefaya: The New Politics in Egypt," *Arab Studies Quarterly*, Vol. 29, No. 1, January 2007, pp. 39–60.

Solidaire sans Frontieres, "Stop Political Trials by the Military in Egypt," June 6, 2007. As of September 27, 2007:
http://www.europe-solidaire.org/spip.php?article6244

Stephens, Bret, "With Friends Like This: Bush Betrays Egypt's Democrats, for What?" *Wall Street Journal*, June 4, 2006. As of January 30, 2008:
http://online.wsj.com/article/SB114894836307965830.html?mod=opinion_main_commentaries

Tackaberry, John, "Egypt: Continuing Arrest of Critics and Opponents 'Chill' Prospects for Reform," Amnesty.ca, May 27, 2005. As of September 27, 2007:
http://www.amnesty.ca/resource_centre/news/view.php?load=arcview&article=2497&c=Resource+Centre+News

Tarabishi, George, *On the Culture of Democracy* [*fi thaqafat al-dimuqratiyya*], Beirut, Lebanon: Dar al-Talica Publishing, 1998.

U.S. Department of State, Daily Press Briefing, May 11, 2006. As of January 30, 2008:
http://www.state.gov/r/pa/prs/dpb/2006/66163.htm

"US State Secretary Cancels Trip to Egypt," *People's Daily Online*, February 27, 2005. As of February 1, 2008:
http://english.people.com.cn/200502/27/eng20050227_174845.html

Wehda Masrya, "A Call for a Protestation," n.d. As of September 26, 2007:
http://wa7damasrya.blogspot.com/

"Weak Turnout for the Referendum of the Constitutional Amendments in Egypt ['iqbal dacif cala istifta' al-tacdilat al-dusturiyya fi misr]," Alghad.jo, n.d. As of April 13, 2007:
http://www.alghad.jo

Weisman, Steven R., "Rice Urges Egyptians and Saudis to Democratize," *New York Times*, June 21, 2005. As of January 30, 2008:
http://www.nytimes.com/2005/06/21/international/middleeast/21rice.html

"What Happened in Cairo? [madha hasal fi al-qahira?]," Beirut.indymedia.org, May 25, 2005. As of May 24, 2007:
http://beirut.indymedia.org/ar/2005/05/2707.shtml

The White House, "President Bush Discusses Freedom in Iraq and Middle East: Remarks by the President at the 20th Anniversary of the National Endowment for Democracy," press release, November 6, 2003. As of January 30, 2008:
http://www.whitehouse.gov/news/releases/2003/11/20031106-2.html

———, "President Bush, Egyptian President Mubarak Meet with Reporters," press release, April 12, 2004. As of January 30, 2008:
http://www.whitehouse.gov/news/releases/2004/04/20040412-3.html

"Why Has Its Popularity Declined? Kefaya—Between the Illnesses of the Opposition and Receiving Blows from Security [limadha tarajacat shacbiyyatuha? kefaya bayna 'amrad al-mucarada wa talaqqi al-darabat al-'amniyya]," Daralhayat.com, June 7, 2007. As of June 14, 2007:
http://www.daralhayat.com/special/issues/06-2007/Item-20070607-072211c7-c0a8-10ed-01b1-699670b86def/story.html

Yahya, Ayman, "The Phenomenon of Egyptian Strikes [thahirat al-'idrabat al-misriyya]," Alwaqt.com, May 21, 2007. As of May 24, 2007:
http://www.alwaqt.com/blogprint.php?baid=3433

Youssef, Mohammed, "Has Kefaya Lost Its Way and Entered the History Museum? [hal dallat harakat Kefaya wa dakhalat mathaf al-tarikh]," Rezgar.com, March 3, 2007. As of October 29, 2007:
http://www.rezgar.com/debat/show.art.asp?aid=91389

Zaki, Mina, "The End," Kefaya7aram.blogspot.com, March 3, 2007a. As of September 27, 2007:
http://Kefaya7aram.blogspot.com/search?q=%D9%83%D9%81%D8%A7%D9%8A%D8%A9

———, "Mubarak Began His Preemptive Strikes on the Opposition for Obliterating His Constitutional Distortions," Kefaya7aram.blogspot.com, 2007b. As of September 26, 2007:
http://Kefaya7aram.blogspot.com/2007/03/blog-post_25.html.